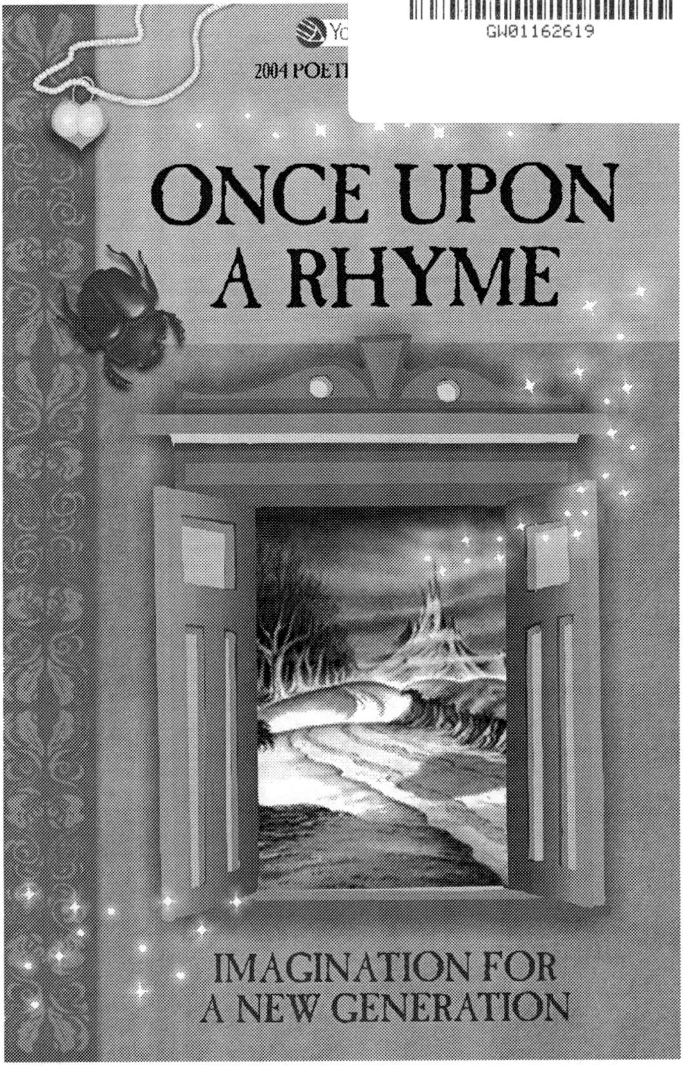

Staffordshire

Edited by Chris Hallam

YoungWriters
First published in Great Britain in 2004 by:
Young Writers
Remus House
Coltsfoot Drive
Peterborough
PE2 9JX
Telephone: 01733 890066
Website: www.youngwriters.co.uk

SB ISBN 1 84460 454 3

Foreword

Young Writers was established in 1991 and has been passionately devoted to the promotion of reading and writing in children and young adults ever since. The quest continues today. Young Writers remains as committed to engendering the fostering of burgeoning poetic and literary talent as ever.

This year's Young Writers competition has proven as vibrant and dynamic as ever and we are delighted to present a showcase of the best poetry from across the UK. Each poem has been carefully selected from a wealth of *Once Upon A Rhyme* entries before ultimately being published in this, our twelfth primary school poetry series.

Once again, we have been supremely impressed by the overall high quality of the entries we have received. The imagination, energy and creativity which has gone into each young writer's entry made choosing the best poems a challenging and often difficult but ultimately hugely rewarding task - the general high standard of the work submitted amply vindicating this opportunity to bring their poetry to a larger appreciative audience.

We sincerely hope you are pleased with our final selection and that you will enjoy *Once Upon A Rhyme Staffordshire* for many years to come.

Contents

The Poems

Toastie Ghostie

Creeping down the corridor,
Through the magic door,
Entering into a sixth floor,
When suddenly I heard a roar,

I took a step to the left, a step to the right,
When suddenly I had a fright,
I turned around and saw a ghost,
Offering me some magic toast.

Jacob Matthews (10)

My Pal

Hair is like a blonde string.
Head is like a rounded heart.
Eyes like smooth, glittering balls.
Nose like a pointing arrow.
Mouth like a rubber ring.
Lips as red as the sun.
Voice is like a booming call.
Breath like a boiling hot pan.
Teeth like sharp shark teeth.
Ears like circle shapes.
Neck like a long, thick tube.
Body like a whale baby.
Heart like a telephone ringing.
Arms like branches on trees.
Hands like a water bottle.
Legs like wires on a TV.
Feet like pencil cases.
Toes like handlebars on a bike.

Kimberley Baird (9)
All Saints' CE (C) Primary School

Jonny Wilkinson Kennings

Ball-kicker,
Big-hitter,
Air's-bitter,
Running-quicker,
Glory-sniffer,
Penalty-kicker,
Ball-spinner,
Try-winner.

Ben Cassidy (10)
All Saints' CE (C) Primary School

Jealousy

J ealousy can be about a lot of matters
E veryone else's dress is great but yours is in tatters
A ll of your friends have a partner in the line
L iving life seems hard when everyone else seems fine
O ut of groups in PE
U sually everyone wants to be friends with me
S piteful acts can occur
Y es, jealousy is the green-eyed monster.

Lauren Jenkins (10)
All Saints' CE (C) Primary School

Breathless

You're taking the penalty to win the match,
Your heart is beating,
There's an itch you want to scratch,
You kick, it's going to miss, it swerves in
And you win the match.

Costas Marcou (11)
All Saints' CE (C) Primary School

Listen - Cinquain

Listen,
The thunderstorm,
The rain hammering down,
Denting rooftops all over town,
Listen!

Maddison Saunders-Barker (11)
All Saints' CE (C) Primary School

Flowers

Flowers are sweet, flowers are pretty
Flowers grow in spring but they look better in summer.
When it comes to autumn, they've all gone brown
And when it comes to winter, they've all gone down.

If you go to the park in the summer or spring
You will see lots of flowers playing in the grass.
Daffodils, roses and lavender are the best flowers I have ever seen.

Some flowers are good, some flowers are mean.
My mummy and daddy love flowers like me.
Have you ever had the thought that flowers wee?
That's all I know about flowers for now but I bet tomorrow
I will know more!

Katy Henman (8)
All Saints' CE (C) Primary School

What's That? - Cinquain

What's that?
Is it the wind?
Is it the tree branches
Creaking, cracking, snapping, breaking . . . ?
What's that?

Faye Brant (11)
All Saints' CE (C) Primary School

I Wish

I wish
I wish I could fly, fly high . . .
Above in the blue sky,
I wish,
I wish,
Soaring up above the buildings . . .
I wish,
I wish.

Jack Flavell (10)
All Saints' CE (C) Primary School

Cargoes

A giant German car ferry,
Coming from Hamburg,
Lashing through the Channel,
In the jazzy July days,
With a cargo of vehicles,
Caravans and lorries,
Scooters and bikes and Mercedes.

Christopher Anthony Simms (10)
All Saints' CE (C) Primary School

Kennings Cat

Mouse-killer.
Life-fulfiller.
Alley-walker.
Butterfly-stalker.
Body-licker.
Cotton-kicker.

Jake Dumolo Ralley (10)
All Saints' CE (C) Primary School

Breathless

Blue water,
Repeating,
Cold waves,
Becoming louder,
Arms restless,
Feet dawdling,
Breath runs out,
Heart pumps quickly.
Underwater animals
Go by my face,
Breathing bubbles,
Legs go kick, kick.

White water,
Rapidly,
White horses
Galloping,
Slow movement,
No oxygen,
No breath,
H_2O everywhere,
No air,
No human life,
People drowning.

Amelia Felton (10)
All Saints' CE (C) Primary School

A Noose - Kennings

Neck breaker,
Death maker.
Life ender,
Body bender.
Crime killer,
Blood spiller.

David Cleary (10)
All Saints' CE (C) Primary School

A Viper - Kennings

Slimy-slitherer
Human-witherer
Hole-hider
Mouse-finder
Tree-climber
Branch-binder
Fang-fighter
Coiled-striker.

Jack Walford (10)
All Saints' CE (C) Primary School

An Ocean - Kennings

Fish-flipper
Wave-bringer
Boat-wearer
Rock-crusher
Sun-catcher
Bird-carrier
Wind-wailer
Speedboat-sailor.

Emma Rutter (11)
All Saints' CE (C) Primary School

Windigo

W ild and fierce, he wanders by will.
I ndependently alone, he creeps to kill.
N ew things like nature startle him.
D ead one day, he will lie with bugs all over him.
I ce all around makes him slip.
G oing splat on the floor, he's OK.
'O w!' he roars all the way.

Alice Brown (8)
All Saints' CE (C) Primary School

My Monster Dad

Hair as grey as rain clouds
Brain as small as a flea
Clothes as boring as homework
Arms as hairy as a spider
Legs as long as tree branches
Eats as much as a pig would
Socks as smelly as mouldy cheese
Snores as loud as an express train
Nose as long as Pinocchio's
Breath as smelly as rotten eggs
Eyes as bright as headlamps
Eyebrows as thick as bushes
Eyelashes as long as grass
Sneezes as loud as thunder
My dad mopes around the house all day
He's a hopeless case
But I love him anyway.

Bethan Moss (9)
All Saints' CE (C) Primary School

Red

Softly soaring, now the sun,
Climbs the sky in heralding fun;
Up and up and seeping wide
She spreads her glow in her stride.
Across the reddening, rosy trees,
Crimson fields and farms she sees,
People see her red rays pounce,
She dyes bricks red on every house.
On the window she lays her red glare,
As she creeps silently through the air.

Vicky Swash (11)
All Saints' CE (C) Primary School

My Dad's Amazing!

My dad's *amazing* for he can . . .

Make mountains out of molehills,
Teach Granny to suck eggs,
Make Mum's blood boil and drive her up the wall.

My dad's *amazing* for he can . . .

Walk around upside down,
Do forward flips in sinking sand,
Pop a drum in a big brass band,
My dad's god and he's the man of the land.

My dad's *amazing* for he can . . .

Dance on the roof,
Fly like a bird
With a cow on his head.

My dad's *amazing* and he's the best!

Sophie Laing
All Saints' CE (C) Primary School

The Listeners

(Based on 'The Listeners' by Walter De La Mare)

And as the traveller rode away
'Neath the starry sky,
Wondering if he'd enter here another day,
To repeat his desperate cry

And while the hooves were pattering
Down the hateful hill,
The blanket of silence was returned,
And all was silent and still.

Caroline Dwyer (10)
All Saints' CE (C) Primary School

That's What I Call Relaxing

Breezy wind, hot sun and some girls sucking their thumbs,
Birds singing in the background,
That's what I call relaxing.

Sea going up the shore and me swimming in the pool.
Someone playing with some cards,
That's what I call relaxing.

Joe's getting shells and Mom's got a tan.
Dad's gone snorkelling,
That's what I call relaxing.

Now we have our tea, done a lot of dancing.
I feel very sleepy, I have fallen asleep,
That's what I call relaxing.

Charlie Parry (8)
All Saints' CE (C) Primary School

Pluto The Dog

Imagine a head as big as a water bottle.
A nose like a sausage.
A collar like a piece of green string.
Teeth like sharp swords.
Ears as black as the sky at night.
Skin as yellow as the sun.
Eyes as blue as the interactive whiteboard.
A bone as white as snow.
A collar-piece as silver as the brightest star.
A tail as long as a spider's leg.

Myles Elliot Sedgwick (8)
All Saints' CE (C) Primary School

Gold And Silver

Gold is Christmas,
All over the tree,
Tinsel and baubles,
And presents for me.
There are bows and ribbons,
Which look very neat,
And chocolate coins,
Yummy to eat.

Silver in the kitchen,
The knives and forks,
Saucepan and the kettle
Are shiny of course.
The toaster in the corner,
The door handles shine,
The silver tap drips,
That spoon is mine.

Gold and silver
Are hot and cold,
A hot summer's day,
Then a sunset of gold.
The silver stars
Twinkle all night long,
A cold, frosty morning
And the birds sing a song.

Laura Groves (8)
All Saints' CE (C) Primary School

Gold And Silver

Gold is the sun,
That's high in the sky,
Gold is wheat,
Ready for harvest,
Gold is a coin,
That tings on the floor,
Gold is tinsel,
That glows in the dark.

Silver is foil,
That crinkles with shine,
Silver is a whisk,
That twirls in the bowl,
Silver is the bracelet,
That sparkles on my wrist,
Silver is an earring,
That shines on my ear.

Gold is a candle,
That shines in the night,
Gold is an eagle,
That flies in the sky,
Gold is a brooch,
It is like a badge,
Gold is a locket,
That you can open up.
You look in the mirror
And it shines your life up.

Chloe Marcou (8)
All Saints' CE (C) Primary School

Imagine!

Imagine a snail,
as big as a whale

Imagine a cat,
as small as a rat

Imagine a chair,
as big as a bear

Imagine a bat
as big as a cat

Imagine a mouse,
as big as a house

Imagine a pen,
as big as a hen,

Imagine Jordan
winning the competition!

Jordan Taylor (8)
All Saints' CE (C) Primary School

Mouldy Man

Hair as short as whiskers.
Eyes as big as balls.
Teeth as sharp as blades.
Nails as yellow as the sun.
Body like a square box.
Legs as thin as ice.
Ears as red as fire.
Fingers as long as lightning.
Nose shaped like a pyramid.

Rebecca Wood
All Saints' CE (C) Primary School

Imagine!

Imagine an ant as big as an elephant
Imagine Dale as small as a snail
Imagine hail as large as a great white whale
Imagine a mouse as large as a house
Imagine Ben as real as a hen
Imagine a bin as big as an inn
Imagine a moose as small as a goose
Imagine a fox as big as a box
Imagine Mike as large as a bike
Imagine Shaun as small as a prawn
Imagine a cub as big as a pub
Imagine Dean as small as a baked bean
Imagine a rat as flat as a mat.

Lauren Fox (8)
All Saints' CE (C) Primary School

Monkeys

Monkey, monkey, can you see
The gliding monkeys swinging in the tree?
Monkey, monkey, can you smell
The lovely smell of bananas?
Monkey, monkey, can you see
Their pointy hair,
And their fluffy long tails,
Their burning hands from gripping the trees
And their wet, sweaty noses from the sun?
Monkey, monkey, say goodbye.

Jack Roddick (7)
All Saints' CE (C) Primary School

Cats Can Be . . .

Cats can be big
Cats can be small
Cats can rest their head on a bed
Cats can scratch
Cats can snatch
Cats can have fur
Or be a him or a her!
Cats can like food
Some can be in a mood
They can be really nice
And eat lots of mice!
Cats can be kind
Cats can be fluffy
I love cats
So does my mummy!

Rosie Smith (8)
All Saints' CE (C) Primary School

Imagine

Imagine a cake
as big as a lake.
Imagine a hare
as big as a bear.
Imagine a dog
as big as a bog.
Imagine a hen
as big as men.
Imagine a cat
as thin as a mat.

Isobel Felton (8)
All Saints' CE (C) Primary School

Gold

Gold is a coin,
clinking and clanking
in my pocket.

Gold is a piece of tinsel
twinkling and bright
on the Christmas tree.

Gold is an apple,
crunchy and crisp.

Gold is a candle,
flickering with light.

Gold is a wand,
turning people into frogs.

Gold is a bowl
with crunchy nut cereal in it.

Gold is a car
taking us to Heaven.

Gold is the Leaning Tower of Pisa
positioned with pride.

Gold is the sun
gleaming with glory.

Thomas Edward Bacon (8)
All Saints' CE (C) Primary School

Alien

Hair like slimy spaghetti
Head like a big balloon
Eyes like the blue sea
Nose as long as Pinocchio's
Mouth like red-hot fire
Lips as thick as sausages
Voice as deep as a swimming pool!

Ria Whyman (8)
All Saints' CE (C) Primary School

A Girl's World

A rose is red,
A bluebell is blue,
The grass is green,
A pink flower!
A pansy is pretty,
A weed is annoying,
The seaweed is salty,
A yellow flower!
A dancing school,
A blue, blue sky,
The orange sun,
A girl's world.

Kathryn Gee (8)
All Saints' CE (C) Primary School

Imagine!

Imagine a toy
as big as a boy.
Imagine a frog
as big as a dog.
Imagine a mat
as soft as a cat.
Imagine a hen
as still as a pen.
Imagine a key
as blue as the sea!

Jasmine Burr (8)
All Saints' CE (C) Primary School

That's What I Call *Relaxing!*

Reading a book,
In a quiet place,
Away from my sister,
That's what I call relaxing.

My Uncle Mike,
Has a Jaguar,
The smell of leather seats,
That's what I call relaxing.

Listening to music,
Lying on my bed,
On my cuddly duvet,
That's what I call relaxing.

Sitting on the soft sofa,
Snuggled with my family,
Watching a DVD,
That's what I call relaxing.

On Bantham beach,
When it is summer,
While it's warm and quiet,
That's what I call relaxing.

When I'm outside,
Where there's a gentle breeze,
And I'm sitting on my bench,
That's what I call relaxing.

Listening to water,
Trickling down a stream,
It's so lovely and gentle,
That's what I call relaxing.

Thomas Peach (9)
All Saints' CE (C) Primary School

Dead Tunes

Here lies a body of a ten-year-old
who did not do as he was told.

Here lies a body of a lonely child
selfish, reckless, shameless, wild.

Here lies a body of a worn out dad
driven by his kids, crazy, mad.

Here lies a body of a worn out mum
worked to the bone, tired of moans,
kind of glum.

Thomas Gore (8)
All Saints' CE (C) Primary School

My Dog Sam

My Sam is furry,
And he's small,
And he's funny.

Sam is fast,
And he can bark,
And he can swim.

And I love Sam,
And I will play with him,
And will run with him.

Shaun Prince (8)
All Saints' CE (C) Primary School

The Sun

The sun is bright
The sun is light
The sun sleeps in the night.

The sun lives in the sky
The sun lives really, really high.

The sun is yellow
The sun is red.

The sun is flames
The sun is fire.

Matthew Reilly (7)
All Saints' CE (C) Primary School

The Sun

The sun is as bright as a star.
The sun shines like the moon.
The sun sparkles in the sky.
The sun is warmer than a fire.
The sun is a great big ball of flames.
The sun is opposite of the moon.
The sun shines by day and sleeps at night.
The sun can kill anything that touches it.
The sun brightens up a dull, dull day.

Michael Jonathan Mander (7)
All Saints' CE (C) Primary School

What About The *Monkeys?*

A lligators in the water. What about the monkeys?
B irds flying like aeroplanes. What about the monkeys?
C ats miaowing all around. What about the monkeys?
D ogs woofing, *'Woof, woof.'* What about the monkeys?
E lephants stomp all around. What about the monkeys?
F ish blob, *'Blob, blob, blob.'* What about the monkeys?
G iraffes lick anything. What about the monkeys?
H ippos turn pink in water. What about the monkeys?
I guanas sleep all day. What about the monkeys?
J aguars, yellow and black. What about the monkeys?
K oalas, soft and smooth. What about the monkeys?
L ions roar, *'Roar, roar, roar!'* What about the monkeys?
N its bite your hair. What about the monkeys?
O ctopus swing their arms. What about the monkeys?
P andas, black and white. What about the monkeys?
Q ueen Bee, *'Buzz!'* What about the monkeys?
R abbits poo, *'Plop.'* What about the monkeys?
S nakes *'Sssss.'* What about the monkeys?
T urtles, big shell. What about the monkeys?
U nicorns in Heaven. What about the monkeys?
V ixen is a girl fox. What about the monkeys?
W hales, as long as a country. What about the monkeys?
eX tra large elephant. What about the monkeys?
Y ak, shaggy-haired ox. What about the monkeys?
Z ebras, black and white. What about the monkeys?
M onkeys, phew the long lasting monkeys.

Joe Tilley (8)
All Saints' CE (C) Primary School

Here Come The Monkeys

Monkeys are fun,
They're asleep,
They're awake.

Here come the monkeys,
They're swinging near,
They might scare you if you're there.

Here come the monkeys,
They're big and bold,
They're black and brown.

Here come the monkeys,
They're amazing,
They scream all day.

Here come the monkeys,
They're sleeping because it's night,
They're hiding because of poachers.

Here come the monkeys,
They're coming near,
To defend, you hear.

Here come the monkeys,
They're upside down,
They're coming for a drink, crocodile!

Georgia Bradley (7)
All Saints' CE (C) Primary School

Colours

Red is for the Russian sun,
Yellow is for the shining stars,
Pink is for the dancing flowers,
Green is for the wavy grass,
Ruby is for my sparkling ring.

What would we do without
Colours?

Chloe Chapman (8)
All Saints' CE (C) Primary School

Ten Things I Found In A Wizard's Pocket . . .

A cat as a big as a dinosaur
A giant plant with gold at the top
A chest that gives you gold
A dog that talks
A coffin
A cat that climbs the beanstalk
A mountain
A pencil that writes by itself
A magic ring that opens every door
A tree as big as a palace.

Christie Buxton-Hopley (8)
All Saints' CE (A) Primary School

Winter

Winter creeps in without a sound,
Blankets of snow cover the ground.
Children play in the snow,
Making their faces really glow.

The icy winds swirl through the trees,
Makes the ponds and rivers freeze.
The days are short, the nights are long,
But the little robin still sings his song.

Rebecca England (10)
All Saints' CE (A) Primary School

There Was An Old Women of Paris

There was an old woman of Paris
Who liked doing the jig by the sea
She wore a man's kilt
With her hat on a tilt,
That weird old woman of Paris.

Lauren-Nicole Clewley (9)
All Saints' CE (A) Primary School

Ten Things Found In A Wizard's Pocket

A magic chocolate bar which lasts forever
A football that teaches you how to play
An owl that talks
An invisible jumper
A fish that can talk
An instrument that plays by itself
A talking dog
A magic pen
A bed that wakes you up in the morning
Sweets that keep changing colour.

Luke Robinson (8)
All Saints' CE (A) Primary School

Family Zoo

My mom is like a dolphin
As graceful as can be
My dad is like a lion
How scary he can be
My nan is like a dog
Who barks if I do something wrong
My grandad is like a monkey
Who's cheeky that's for sure
But me, I'm the odd one out
And I'm always monkeying around.

Seona Louise Pearce (10)
All Saints' CE (A) Primary School

My Family Poem

My mum is a beautiful flower, as pretty as a princess.
My dad is a wrestler, big, muscly and tough.
My sister is a caterpillar eating too much.
My brother is a little deer investigating and getting into trouble.
Me? I'm a bunny stuck inside all day with nothing to play with.

Megan Robinson (10)
All Saints' CE (A) Primary School

The Animal House

I have a bear, a big cuddly bear
She looks after me and gets the food ready
I call her Mom.

I have a rhino
He's fast and sometimes kind
I call him Dad.

I have a guinea pig
She's small and mad and she talks a lot
I call her my sister.

I have a dog, a very helpful dog
She's kind and she looks after me
I call her Nan.

Ellis Brown (9)
All Saints' CE (A) Primary School

Autumn And Winter

A ll the leaves turn different colours.
U mbrellas stop you getting wet.
T he nights go darker earlier.
U sually the animals hibernate.
M eals are warm.
N uts get collected by squirrels.

W rap up warm when it is cold.
I ce on the canal.
N o one wears shorts or a T-shirt.
T emperatures get cold.
E verybody shivers.
R eindeer pull Santa's sleigh.

Jake Robbins (9)
All Saints' CE (A) Primary School

The Animal House

I have a bear, a big black bear
He is strong
He loves cuddles
He is sometimes a bit scary, I call him Daddy

I also have an owl
She gets all the food
She has really good eyesight
She cares for her young, I call her Mummy

I have a kitten
He is sometimes very annoying
But quite cuddly
He loves meat and milk, I call him my brother, George.

I have a dog
She likes running around
She is very playful
She likes walks, I call her Auntie Mary.

Then there's me.
I know what I am
I'm a little warm sparrow.

Judy Goodwin (8)
All Saints' CE (A) Primary School

Ten Things Found In A Wizard's Pocket

A tree that grows chocolate.
A pen that will write on its own.
A September that never comes.
A meeting with other wizards.
A cow that can swim.
An ox that gets you dressed.
A German Shepherd that can talk.
A book that can snore.
A book of spells.
A flying carpet.

Dean Fuggle (7)
All Saints' CE (A) Primary School

Animal Family

I have a mouse
She works all day
And looks after my sisters.
I call her Mum.

I have a lion
He's out most of the day
He gets cross with my sisters.
I call him Dad

I have a monkey
She plays all day
And gets into trouble.
I call her Rachel, my sister.

And then there's me.
I'm a dove.
I put up with them.

Rebecca Wallace (7)
All Saints' CE (A) Primary School

Ten Things Found In A Wizard's Pocket

A very big waterproof clock.
A lot of wands.
The biggest pencil sharpener.
A chocolate tree.
A flying carpet.
An owl that can do your washing up.
A cow that can swim.
A ox that gets dressed.
A hut that can clean itself.
A chocolate bar that can talk.

Harry Sotnick (7)
All Saints' CE (A) Primary School

The Animal House

I have a dragon, a powerful dragon.
He works a lot and is out all day.
He smokes all the time and eats a lot of meat.
He is the best dragon ever. I call him Dad.

I also have a cat.
She works at home all day.
She is soft, cuddly and graceful.
She looks after her young. I call her Mum.

I have a wasp, a big wasp.
He is very annoying.
He is horrible to me and always hurts me.
When he is angry he hurts me a lot.
I call him Matthew, my brother.

I have a fox, a tufty-faced fox.
She's always creeping around.
She's got orange hair and a pointy nose
She's very sneaky. I call her Nan.

And then there's me,
I know what I am.
I'm the koala bear.

Molly Teece (8)
All Saints' CE (A) Primary School

Leaves

Leaves fall down slowly,
Swirling down, down, as they come,
Falling like feathers,
Gliding to the ground,
There they lie, still, motionless.

Dominic Pugh (10)
All Saints' CE (A) Primary School

My Dad

My dad is a bank of clouds
Covering the land,
My dad is a leather jacket
Hard and tough,
My dad is a playful monkey
Playing with me,
My dad is a pouncing dog
Barking all of the time,
My dad is a blue Clio
Driving around the town,
My dad is a wooden chair
Hard to break,
My dad is a crashing wave
Rolling to shore.

Katie Barton (10)
All Saints' CE (A) Primary School

The Seasons

W rap up warm.
I ce skating.
N ot very warm
T asty, warm hot chocolate.
E verybody enjoys Christmas.
R eindeer pull Santa's sleigh.

A nimals get ready for winter.
U mbrellas keep you dry.
T emperature gets cold.
U sually leaves get crispy.
M any leaves fall off the trees.
N uts for squirrels.

Laura Richardson (9)
All Saints' CE (A) Primary School

The Animal House

I have a fox, a fast, strong, cunning fox.
He eats anything and works at night,
I call him Dad.

I also have a giraffe, a tall, quiet, caring giraffe
She likes vegetables and looks after her children,
I call her Mom.

I have a magpie, a smooth, cunning magpie,
He steals my things without me knowing,
I call him Brother.

Then there's me,
I know what I am,
I'm a shark.

Adam Rowe (10)
All Saints' CE (A) Primary School

Winter And Autumn

W arm clothes to wear.
I ce on the ponds and Jack Frost comes.
N uts are collected by squirrels.
T rees are bare.
E llie and Jake have snowball fights.
R ats hibernate.

A utumn leaves are falling off the trees.
U mbrellas to keep dry.
T emperature gets cooler.
U nder the tree we play in piles of leaves.
M ice get ready to hibernate.
N ice cool breeze in my hair.

Ellie Miller (7)
All Saints' CE (A) Primary School

Midnight Fright

Last night I was scared,
I heard something weird,
A crunching, a scampering,
Then a shadow appeared.

I let out a scream,
But nobody spoke,
Nobody jumped,
Nobody woke.

I closed my eyes,
So they were tight,
Hoping that nothing
Would give me a fright.

Why can't those monsters
Just be nice?
Those dirty, terrible,
Sneaky mice.

Alice Le Page (11)
All Saints' CE (A) Primary School

My Mum

My mum is a horse looking after her colts.
My mum is a caring dolphin when I'm feeling ill.
My mum is a roaring lion when I fight with other cubs.
My mum is a sun when she is proud of her stars.
My mum is a rolling wave coming on up to me.
My mum is a lilac Mercedes carrying me round.
My mum is a heart-shaped shortbread because she is easily heartbroken.
My mum is a woolly jumper to cuddle me up in.

Sophie Smith (10)
All Saints' CE (A) Primary School

Seasons

W e wrap up warm with scarves and hats.
I n winter leaves fall off trees.
N ets are put away in the loft.
T he snow lies out on your lawn.
E verybody eats warm food.
R abbits keep warm by running around.

A utumn leaves are crispy.
U mbrellas go up when you go to town.
T he bears hibernate.
U neasily snow bites you.
M ud sticks to your boots.
N ights get dark and cold.

S un is getting warmer.
P lants are growing in the garden.
R ed roses are coming.
I n the spring lambs are born.
N ights are getting warmer.
G ood animals are around.

S un is getting very hot.
U mbrellas are put away.
M usic from the birds appears.
M ums are getting busy round town.
E ating is getting cooler.
R eaders go to the libraries more.

Lauren Becker (7) & Olivia Preston (8)
All Saints' CE (A) Primary School

Friends

Friends are important,
It's nice to have a few,
Whenever there's a problem,
They always comfort you.

Victoria Jackson (10)
Birds Bush Primary School

Night Has Come To *Life!*

She creeps in with her horrible cackle,
As the world changes to a mysterious place.
She's like a bullet from a gun,
Sneaking quickly, making everyone scared.

Silently moving, disturbing everyone's rest,
She's like a burglar stealing everyone's dreams.
She knows you're in your lonely place,
Here she comes into my room, there is no time to run . . .

Kirsty Sands (10)
Birds Bush Primary School

Snowing

S now brings delight
N ow everything is bright,
O h, what a sight,
W onderland of white,
I n the middle of the night,
N ow tucked up in bed so tight,
G listening in the moonlight.

Grace Clarke (8)
Birds Bush Primary School

Rachael

She's the joker in the pack,
She's the imp on my shoulder,
Though sometimes she arches like a tree
And is as busy as a bee,
Her eyes are as blue as the sky,
She's as bright as a sunflower,
And she smells as sweet as a rose.

Rachel Elizabeth Atkins (10)
Birds Bush Primary School

My Best Friend

She's a soft chair
She's a tall giraffe
A light yellow, juicy lemon
A morning person jumping out of bed
A tall, yellow sunflower
She's a disco, dancing all night
She's a falcon bird.

Lauren Roden (9)
Birds Bush Primary School

My Friend

She's a bouncy blow-up chair,
A library full of books,
The lovely smell of roses,
A huge bowl of ice cream,
A warm summer's day,
She's a wise owl,
And a relaxing room with a hot fire.

Rebecca Timson (10)
Birds Bush Primary School

Crystal Ling

The chief defect of Crystal Ling
She poked her tongue while whistling
Her tongue stuck out, it look so pink
The people stared and had to blink
The noise was louder than a gun
She thought that it was so much fun.

Daniela Ardin (10)
Birds Bush Primary School

Night

When you see Night she's got bright blue eyes
And golden sunshine hair.
Her lips are as red as the red, red rose.
She's like a twinkle of a star.
Her dress is real silk and pure white.

She swoops around, as silent as a tortoise
And moves as quickly as a cheetah.
Night goes through one ear and out the other
Very slowly and turns into night
And creeps around your room.
Do you think she's coming or do you think she's *not?*

Danielle Cairns (10)
Birds Bush Primary School

Annie Chum

The chief defect of Annie Chum
Was swallowing her chewing gum
She swallowed so much she got fat
I don't know what you think of that
She said she didn't, it was lies
I won't be sad if she just dies.

Ciara-Angel Thomas
Birds Bush Primary School

Billy Rose

The tragic tale of Billy Rose
He had his fingers up his nose.
He could not get them out.
His father tried with one big clout.
His fingers were stuck up his nose.
That was the end of Billy Rose.

Ashley Deville (10)
Birds Bush Primary School

The Benevolent Type Of Night

Night, gentle and bright,
More dazzling than the speedy stars.
He is like a lustrous angel,
Who swiftly moves now and then,
His big, blue eyes which give him away,
And his huge, bulky arms which constantly protect me.

It's 10.30pm, time for bed,
He enters his grandson's room,
The smell of lavender hovers around,
The child stirs, Night watches over him,
Making sure he's safe and sound,
He sleeps well, Night will be back tomorrow.

Stephen Lees (10)
Birds Bush Primary School

Nightmares

Night is the cause of my unrest.
Hardly breathing, quietly creeping up,
Petrifying its victim with cold, black eyes,
And it begins to talk in a cold rattling voice,
'Drop into slumber, close your eyes,
You're feeling tired and goodnight.'
I know of this because I've seen it,
Lost among the moonlit streets,
Speeding aimlessly this way and that.
Then I saw the horrific scene.
I was even too scared to dare to shout,
Really, it was a nightmare!

Stuart March (11)
Birds Bush Primary School

Rachel

She is as funny as a joke book,
She's a bright red poppy,
She's as busy as a bee
She is as small as a mouse,
She's a little devil,
Her eyes are as brown as a piece of chocolate
She smells as fresh as newly cut grass.

Rachael Parfitt (10)
Birds Bush Primary School

The Tragic Tale Of Barry Bud

The tragic tale of Barry Bud
He was always covered in mud
One day he got stuck by surprise
He felt mud go into his eyes
He could not see
He went so blind
His way around he could not find.

Howard Jones (10)
Birds Bush Primary School

The Tragic Tale of Philip Woo

The tragic tale of Philip Woo
He spent an hour on the loo
All his bits fell in the can
He never will become a man
They went into a different place
They went into outer space.

Robert Horton (10)
Birds Bush Primary School

Finding A Home

Cold, wet, lonely, sad, fierce, afraid,
This is how I was when I didn't have a home.

A broken building was where I slept,
I scavenged for food.

I kept away from people, they were cruel,
Throwing stones and shouting at me.

My fur was dusty as coal, my, I ran with fear!
I was thin and ill, I howled as I prowled around.

Then one day I found a bowl of food for me!
People who spoke gently to me, could it be true?

For years I came closer but would not come in,
Then finally I thought, *why not be happy?*

Now I live with my new family, I am warm and dry,
I have friends.
I am happy.

I am home.

Callum Yates (10)
Bishop Rawle CE Primary School

The Attic Kid

Up the crooked stairs I go, turn the wooden handle,
All I hear is the strike of a match as I light the candle,
Look around, I spot a box, wipe away the dust,
The words appear nice and clear, open it I must.
Peel away the Sellotape, off comes the lid,
I look inside, what do I find? This picture of a kid.

I wake up to find it's all a dream, or is this real what I have seen?
This mystery is still unsolved, the name of the kid has
never been told!

Reagan Twigge (10)
Bishop Rawle CE Primary School

The Sun Comes Up

The sun comes up above the hills
Children playing by the mills,
Watching how the sun shines down
Making shadows on the ground.
Golden beams behind the clouds
People coming in big crowds,
To see the sun shine on their faces
And light up all the darkest places.
Cats and dogs look up above
To see the snow-white flying doves,
The sun behind the snowy mountains
Glistens on the water fountains.
People drinking in the square
From the cool fresh water there,
The sun is warm up in the sky
It spits of fire, no one knows why,
It sets until another day
We're sad it has to go away.

Sophie Taylor (10)
Bishop Rawle CE Primary School

The Gate Of Seasons

In summer the gate is like glinting silver,
Dazzling people's eyes as they play in the park.

In winter the gate is like a snowy arch,
Slowly getting drained of snow by people tall and small.

In spring the gate is cold and wet,
Hosed by the melting snow as the sun melts it away.

In autumn the gate is covered in leaves,
As the trees die from the freezing weather.

All year round the gate is joyful, as remains the park,
So people who are passing by shall never, never cry.

Nathan Emery (10)
Bishop Rawle CE Primary School

Winter Or Summer?

Winter or summer
Oh! Which one to choose?
I love the snow in winter
And summer I don't want to lose,
As it brings the warm sun
And a lot of fun.

As we sit on the beach
And the sun's out of reach
But brings such a warm delight.

In winter there is a sheet of white
Over the fields that once were so green,
The snowmen all over town are
Such a lovely sight.

Ellen Ball (10)
Bishop Rawle CE Primary School

Swimming At The Pool

Deep end, shallow end, it doesn't matter
Surfing, diving, all the lot
Splashing, playing, having fun
Treading water on the spot

Breaststroke, backstroke
Whatever your favourite
You can do at the pool
You can even go with the school

Diving under water with your daughter
Swimming in-between their legs and feet
Floating, stretching on the water
Swimming fun is hard to beat.

Jessica Lovatt (10)
Bishop Rawle CE Primary School

The Day I Shrunk!

That day I shrunk down like a fly,
I waved my family and friends goodbye.
I looked across the living room,
I knew I was going to walk to my doom.
The chairs looked like a mighty house,
And I looked like a tiny mouse.
It was a nice day,
My friends were out to play,
But I met someone on my way.
It was so scary,
It was so hairy,
It said to me, 'Hey kid, you're free, run around like me.'
I ran and jumped on a magic square,
That floated me into thin air.
I was there,
I was big!
'Thank you Mister Spider.'

Isobelle Jade Seaton (10)
Bishop Rawle CE Primary School

My Favourite Teddy Bear

My favourite teddy sits up there,
It gives me comfort when I'm there.
It always has a soft embrace,
When I put it on my face.

I look into his eyes,
Oh, he is so wise!
He stares at me with open arms,
I'm taken with his charms.

I love my favourite teddy bear,
And I know that he cares.
He's always waiting up there for me,
And that's the way it will always be.

Daniel Gosling (10)
Bishop Rawle CE Primary School

My Budgie

I love my little budgie
She's green, yellow and black,
But if I leave a door wide open
I'm afraid she'll never come back.

She lives in a dome-shaped cage
With food, mirrors and toys,
And tweets ever so loud
Whenever there is a noise.

She likes to watch the telly
She likes to fly around,
Up to her favourite place
Is where she can be found.

I love my little budgie
And I think if she could,
She'd tell me that she loves me too
That really would be good.

Alec Stubbs
Bishop Rawle CE Primary School

The Butterfly

The prettiest fly is a butterfly,
She flies so high in the sky,
You can't see her, you can't hear her,
She'll hide in your flowers,
And dance around your garden,
She's so fast you will never catch her,
She'll fly right past,
She's got lots of colours on her beautiful wings,
She looks better than anything,
She's as light as a feather,
And as swift as a bird,
She's the most gorgeous thing in the whole wide world.

Katie Sims (10)
Bishop Rawle CE Primary School

The ?

I am slow, slow, slow
As I go, go, go,
All my friends in my class
Are fast, fast, fast,
I am small and slow
And sometimes don't know where to go,
I live in a shell
I will slide up your doorbell,
Some people take me in
But sometimes I end up in a bin,
I eat all your leaves
And gobble up very small trees,
I am kept in a tub
With lots of grubs,
I get crushed and pushed all over the place
And sometimes I even get kicked in the face!
I will slide up your garden chairs
And say all my prayers,
So I won't get crushed, crushed, crushed
And mushed, mushed, mushed,
I leave a trail
So I must be a snail.

Susannah Mycock (10)
Bishop Rawle CE Primary School

You're Perfect

I love you when you're laughing,
I love you when you're sad,
I love you when you're teasing,
I love you when you're mad,
I love you when you're sleeping,
I love you when you're glad,
But I mostly love you
Just because you're *you!*

Rian Perkins (9)
Bower Norris RC Primary School

My Family And Friends

My family loves me, my family cares for me and my family is always there for me.

Besides their work, besides their play, they've always got something nice to say.

They help, they care and they always encourage us to share.

My family is great, they're so friendly and a good mate (except my brother).

My friends are just the same, they've got a heart of gold, no matter who or where you're from, they will always cheer you up to three from one.

When you've been cheered up to three, you'll jump up and shout, 'Yippee!'

My family and friends are the best, I can understand if you don't agree but leave the decision up to me and I will keep them for eternity. I will eventually lose them but I won't be too scared because I will see them up there.

Kerianne Heaton (9)
Bower Norris RC Primary School

The Woods

The woods were haunted . . .
Ghosts hovered in the woods
Vampires sneaked through the woods
Ghouls spied in the woods
Skeletons partied in the woods
I once went in the woods
And never came out
Till this day I woke
With shock!
I was in Heaven!

Rebecca Lyons (9)
Bower Norris RC Primary School

Winter

I am winter, cold and wet,
with the snow falling on the naked trees.
I am full of snow, crispy and white icy snow on my hair.
Winter is so cold and white, I have to wrap up warm and tight.
You must eat something warm and nice,
and then you can go skating on the ice.
You have to wear your gloves, scarf and hat,
so you do not catch your death.
Your death!

Rafal Majewski (10)
Bower Norris RC Primary School

No!

No sun - no moon - *no* afternoon
No world - *no* Earth - *no* twinkling stars
No people - *no* bed - *no* colour
No air - *no* wear - *no* planet called Mars
No dear - *no* tear - *no* one there.

No height - *no* might - *no* light
No right - *no* sight - *no* night
No sleeping - *no* weeping - *no* eating.

Michael Short (9)
Bower Norris RC Primary School

Dentists

I know about your dentist,
You may think he's not nice,
But I think mine's thrice as nice.
I know you bite sometimes,
But if you do not know
That a dentist is your teeth's best friend,
So, bite someone else instead!

Damien Glover (9)
Bower Norris RC Primary School

The Hedgehog

As the autumn breeze,
Blows the brownish leaves,
Off the long, tall trees,
The woodland creatures run around,
Tiny footsteps on the ground.
Tip-tap! Tip-tap! Look at them go!
Tip-tap! Leap! They never go slow!

But when other creatures are in a rush,
The spiky little hedgehog hides in a bush.
You see he is fast asleep,
He will not make a single leap.

Now he lies in his house,
Lying there as quiet as a mouse.
Nothing can distract him, not even a fly,
Until the sunny, spring sun is shining in the sky.

Clodagh Churm (9)
Bower Norris RC Primary School

My Week

Monday, Monday, the start of the week,
Tuesday, Tuesday, history, we weep,
Wednesday, we have PE,
Thursday, ICT,
Friday, Friday, art we do,
Saturday, Saturday, no school, whoopee!
Sunday, Sunday, early to bed,
School in the morning we just dread,
Worst of all is our teacher,
Mr Davis,
With his horrid glare.

Loren Rutherford (10)
Bower Norris RC Primary School

Friends

Short, stinky, fat and tall,
Does not matter,
We'll have a ball.
Short, stinky, fat or tall,
Does not matter,
We are still cool.
Loren is tall, she goes to school,
Fay is fat, she has a ginger cat,
Sarah is stinky, she has a baby pinky
Martha is short, she plays a lot of sport.
Short, stinky, fat and tall.

Ayleshe Smith (9)
Bower Norris RC Primary School

My Best Sports

I'm good at football,
I'm good at hockey,
my mates are very lucky,
we're all in a team
and we all share a dream,
to win for our football team
and then we have custard creams.
Once after that we went to my house
and made a trap for a baby mouse.
My mum told me off so I ran out the house.

Kieron McGrady (9)
Bower Norris RC Primary School

Spring

A snowdrop appears as white as snow and so beautiful,
Animals come out of their sleep to see the world,
Miniature frogs with long legs and perfect breastroke,
The weather's getting warmer,
And new growth awakens,
Insects are flying about like little pests,
Rabbits are hopping,
Children are playing happily,
The winds die away,
Frogs are jumping,
Magically, blossom appears on the trees,
Birds are cheeping in the trees,
All the trees grab back their leaves,
Life starts its wonders all over again,
Badgers and mice come out of their sleep,
Birds peck into the soil and come up with worms,
Worms going in and out of the soil,
Like it is water,
Mice scurrying about in the fields,
Life turns green,
Nests appear in the trees,
Easter draws nearer by the second,
A spike of green appears,
Tadpoles darting about in the ponds,
The sun gleams down,
Daffodils appear so yellow and bright,
Grass so green and lush,
The sky so blue,
The sun so bright,
Spring!

Benjamin Alexander Edge (10)
Bower Norris RC Primary School

The Vampire

The vampire, the vampire, it's scared of the cross,
The vampire, the vampire, it cares not for loss.
The vampire, the vampire, it hates all the light,
The vampire, the vampire, it comes out at night.
The vampire, the vampire, silver burns its skin,
The vampire, the vampire, what it does is a sin.
The vampire, the vampire, it needs blood to survive,
The vampire, the vampire, it's not even alive!

Joseph Collier (9)
Bower Norris RC Primary School

School

Happy times all around school.
Power building up from hard work.
Need to get out of classroom,
For a break!
Bell rings.
Back to work.
People working hard.
All quiet.
Smelling pencil leads.
Tasting plastic of ruler.
Bell rings once again.
End of a hard day.
Looking forward
For a play.
Tired.
Ready for fun.
Hooray! Hooray!

Ashley Allen (9)
Carmountside Primary School

School

Happy times in the school classroom.
Energy used up from the work completed.
Feeling happy, fresh air away from the hot room.
Work starts again!
Hearing good noises.
Seeing my friends joining words.
Doing messier things.
School is finished.
Playing outside school with my friends.
I am so tired.
Ready for my tea.
Bedtime is here.
Watching TV
Before I drift off to sleep!

Ivan Wright (9)
Carmountside Primary School

School

Miserable in school
Energy used up, work done.
Fresh air,
Away from the stuffy classroom.
Work starts again
Bringing more hardness
In the classroom.
Seeing friends when we are
Touching gooey glue sticks.
End of school day.

Reece Conway (9)
Carmountside Primary School

School

Happy times at school.
Work is neat and done.
It's time for play, let's have some fun.
Work is starting!
It needs to be done!
Need to keep the noise down.
Seeing Sir marking work.
Smelling pudding and beans,
Touching horrible glue,
It's time for home.
Pudding for tea.
Time for bed!
Let's have some sleep,
Get ready for the next day.

Danica Craddock (9)
Carmountside Primary School

School

Happy days right ahead.
Away from home, time to work.
On the yard for a break.
Back inside feeling happy.
On a Monday, everyone has a mouth
Like a messy tunnel.
At the end it's great away
From school.
Go home,
But back another day.

Kirsty Hill (10)
Carmountside Primary School

The Hobbit

The Hobbit is the one who lives underground,
The Hobbit does not normally wish to be found.

The Hobbits have really hairy feet,
Young Frodo Baggins, I'd like to meet,

As he is the one who owns Sauron's ring,
Sauron was such an evil king!

Frodo is the friend of Legolas and Gimli,
Both of them in battle, what a sight to see!

Sauron's ring was so evil,
It took over poor little Sméagol!

Now is the time to say goodbye,
Then stand back and watch time fly.

Thomas Geoffrey Longshaw (10)
Carmountside Primary School

School

Great and unhappy times in the schoolyard.
Skill wasted on brilliant work.
Feeling tired at dinner time from the warm classroom.
School starts again.
Smelling glue.
Hearing the teacher talking.
Watching children having fun.
Mouth yawning on Monday.
Touching glue bottles.
Success brings confidence.

Jordan Simcock (8)
Carmountside Primary School

School

Happy times in the classroom.
Energy used up from hard work.
Feeling stiff all over.
Time for fun on the yard.
Go to play in the fresh air
In now.
We go to line up.
Some more work.
Home time.
Having tea.
What a great day!

Chelsea Gordon (9)
Carmountside Primary School

School

Waiting till Friday for football coaching
Work to be done, work to be completed
Energy levels rise up, feeling great
Get some fresh air outside
All getting on
Confidence brings success
Talking as the teacher speaks
Children messing about in class
Teacher annoyed
Nearly time to go home
Going out away from school.

Barry Jones (9)
Carmountside Primary School

School

Cheerful times in the schoolyard.
Everyone used up energy from work completed.
Feeling energy building up.
Fresh air away from the stuffy classroom.
Work all starting again.
Success brings everyone confidence.
Hearing people talking.
Seeing boys and girls working hard.
Touching stinky slimy glue.
Finally school ends.
Playtime at home with friends.
Tired through hard writing.
Ready for food and cheer.

Lucy Beal (9)
Carmountside Primary School

School

Happy times in school
Using energy through the day
Making models in the afternoon
Thinking of the fun and games ahead
Laughing on the yard
In a game of football
Work starts again
Nearly time for home, feeling excited
Going home for food and fun.

Luke Hoddle (9)
Carmountside Primary School

Bullying

Bullying, bullying, it's the worst.
Bullying, bullying, it's like being cursed.
Bullying, bullying, a bang on the nose.
Bullying, bullying, all ripped clothes.
Bullying, bullying, being kicked.
Bullying, bullying, money nicked.
Bullying, bullying, it's like Hell.
Bullying, bullying, a boy got pushed and fell.
Bullying, bullying, this can't go on.
Bullying, bullying, it's stopped and I feel number one.

Joseph Thurston (8)
Carmountside Primary School

School

Happy times in the schoolyard.
Energy used up from work not completed.
Feeling fresh air away from the dusty classroom.
Work starts again!
Smelling pencil leads.
Hearing less noises.
Seeing people working hard.
Mouth yawning.
Touching sticky glue.
Success brings confidence.

Dewayne Jones (8)
Carmountside Primary School

School

Waiting till Friday to make a disco come
Work completed, energy used up
Feeling great when I go outdoors
All working hard
Confidence brings success
Shouting as the teacher speaks
Children running around
Chucking stuff
Smelling sweat
Getting down to work again
Privilege earns disco rewards.
Hooray!

Thomas Alcock (8)
Carmountside Primary School

School

Happy times on the school playground.
Everyone hot and sweaty,
Energy all wasted from the work we have done.
Nice and cool in fresh air,
Away from the hot classroom.
Work starts again, time for maths,
Working so hard, smelling rubber and pencil leads.
End of school, time for home,
Tired and weak, the next day it starts all over again.

Naomi Baskerville (9)
Carmountside Primary School

School

Fun time on the schoolyard.
Losing brain energy as work completed.
Feeling cool away from stuffy heat.
Oh no!
A whole hour of work!
We had to do maths.
I was feeling sleepy.
It's break time again, using up my body energy.
I went in for dinner,
Then outside, had a little more exercise,
Lined up to go back inside,
It's time to do some more work,
After that, home time,
Home and relax!

Richard Barnes (8)
Carmountside Primary School

The Door

(Based on 'The Door' by Miroslav Holub)

Go and open the door.
Maybe there's a floor as flat as a pancake,
A person or an elephant.

Go and open the door.
Maybe there's a giant dinosaur,
Maybe you'll see a puppet or a mouse,
Or a face of a face.

Go and open the door,
Only if there's the lightness blinding.
Even if there's the hollow wind.
Even if there are people there.

Go and open the door.
At least there will be a draught.

Ben Perkins (8)
Dosthill Primary School

The Door

(Based on 'The Door' by Miroslav Holub)

Go and open the door,
There could be a sock,
Or maybe a clock.

Go and open the door,
There could just be something boring,
Maybe just old porridge.

Go and open the door,
Maybe there is nothing at all
Just the silence
At least there will be air
Or a hair or a chair!

Go and open the door!
Go and open the door!

Joe Lombardi (8)
Dosthill Primary School

The Door

(Based on 'The Door' by Miroslav Holub)

Go and open the door
Maybe inside there's a spider as big as a giant
Or a piece of glup as green as grass.

Go and open the door
Maybe you'll hear a dinosaur shouting like an elephant
And some TVs too.

Go and open the door
Maybe there's a dragon breathing fire
Or a star brighter than the sun.

So go and open the door
At least there will be a draught.

Peter Bull (8)
Dosthill Primary School

The Door

(Based on 'The Door' by Miroslav Holub)

Go and open the door
Maybe there's a beach
As bright as a rainbow.

Go and open the door
Maybe there's a Mercedes
Racing like a racing cheetah.

Go and open the door
Maybe there's a jacuzzi hot
And bubbly like a bubbly bath.

Go and open the door
Maybe there's a Sunday dinner
Waiting for me in a mansion.

Go and open the door
Maybe there's a limo,
A long, white limo.

Go and open the door
Maybe there's a flying pig
Flying like a heron.

Go and open the door
Maybe there's a talking horse
Talking like a parrot.

Francesca Hughes (9)
Dosthill Primary School

Quickly

Quickly the wind is blowing towards the big blue sky.
Quickly the rain becomes the angry crying from the sky.
Quickly the black clouds run for rain but soon it will come down.
Quickly the wind has come but soon it will be gone.

Lucy Adney (8)
Dosthill Primary School

The Door

(Based on 'The Door' by Miroslav Holub)

Go and open the door.
Maybe you will
hear an owl
hooting like
a loud
horn.

Go and open the door.
Maybe there's a big
dinosaur with teeth
as sharp as
kitchen
knives.

Go and open the door.
Even if there's
nothing there.
Even if there's
only a hair . . .

Go and open the door!

Eleanor Knight (9)
Dosthill Primary School

Quickly

Quickly the motorbike rushed along the motorway
Quickly the roller coaster shot off into the air
Quickly the rain rushed down from the dark, cloudy sky
Quickly the plane whizzed off into the bright, beautiful, shiny sky
Quickly the twister twisted down the dark, scary street
Quickly the kangaroo hopped to the other side
Quick is the leopard - but the quickest of all is the cheetah.

Lauren Bayliss (8)
Dosthill Primary School

The Door

(Based on 'The Door' by Miroslav Holub)

Go and open the door
Maybe outside there's a ghost or a horse
An eyeball or some sweets.

Maybe there's some eyeballs, red like blood of a man
Maybe you'll hear a unicorn yelping and moaning
Maybe there's a hairy chest, spiky like a prickly flower
Maybe green toenails invading the Earth
Maybe there's a hotel, yellow like the sun and moon.

Go and open the door
Maybe you'll feel the cold
Even if there's just a tree

Go and open the door
Maybe there'll be trick or treaters.

Dylon Barratt (8)
Dosthill Primary School

The Door

(Based on 'The Door' by Miroslav Holub)

Go and open the door,
Maybe there's a castle, tall like the tallest tower,
A beach shining like the sun.

Go and open the door
Maybe there's a swimming pool as deep as the sea,
Maybe there's clothes like super models wear,
Maybe there's snow glistening like a white marble.

Go and open the door,
Maybe there's a pool full of dolphins, as cute as puppies,
Maybe you'll see Bratz like never before,
Maybe you don't see anything.

Go and open the door,
At least you will see something.

Sophie Hartley (9)
Dosthill Primary School

The Door

(Based on 'The Door' by Miroslav Holub)

Go and open the door,
Maybe there's Homer Simpson, fat and chubby like a bowling ball.
Go and open the door,
Maybe there's a dolphin, as cute as can be.
Go and open the door,
Maybe there's a warthog snorting like a pig.
Go and open the door,
Maybe there's snow, glistening like the moon.
Go and open the door,
Maybe there's a dinosaur growling like a bear.
Go and open the door,
Maybe you can feel blood rushing down your face.
Go and open the door,
Maybe there's a dog dancing like a chimp.
Go and open the door,
At least my dog Kizzie will still be there.

Rebecca Hardware (8)
Dosthill Primary School

The Door

(Based on 'The Door' by Miroslav Holub)

Go and open the door,
Maybe there's a McLaren F1, fast like a cheetah.

Go and open the door,
Maybe there's an elephant as big as the Millennium Stadium.

Go and open the door,
Maybe there's a posh hotel as tall as a skyscraper.

Go and open the door,
At least there will be something.

James Thompson (8)
Dosthill Primary School

The Door

(Based on 'The Door' by Miroslav Holub)

Go and open the door,
Maybe there's a celebrity with hair like spaghetti.
Go and open the door,
Maybe there's a horse, fit like a runner.
Go and open the door,
Maybe there's a swimming pool, as big and as deep as the sea.
Go and open the door,
Maybe there's a dog zooming like a car.
Go and open the door,
Maybe there's a rabbit hopping like a pogo stick.
Go and open the door,
Maybe there's a person, like a fast runner.
Go and open the door,
At least the letter box will be there.

Emily Kinson (8)
Dosthill Primary School

The Door

(Based on 'The Door' by Miroslav Holub)

Go and open the door,
Maybe outside there's a unicorn, pretty like a glorious flower,
Maybe you'll see a lion as big as a tall tower,
Maybe there's a kitten playing with a ball, grey as dust on a wall.

Go and open the door,
Maybe there's a rabbit saying hello Paul, louder than a hyena's call,
Maybe you'll see someone shouting to come over,
Maybe she's coming in a Land Rover called Grabbit.

Go and open the door,
At least there'll be a ray of sunlight.

Lauren Boulter (9)
Dosthill Primary School

The Door

(Based on 'The Door' by Miroslav Holub)

Go and open the door
maybe there's a mermaid with a long, purple tail
like purple shells in a sea.

Go and open the door
maybe there's a green spy suit like the fresh, green grass.

Go and open the door
maybe there's a famous dancer with a pink tutu
doing ballet like a beautiful sunset.

Go and open the door
maybe there's a spider with eight legs
and a spooky moth like a haunted house.

Jade Ricketts (9)
Dosthill Primary School

The Door

(Based on 'The Door' by Miroslav Holub)

Go and open the door
Maybe there's a yellow crown as yellow as sand
Maybe there's a rollercoaster ride slithering like a snake.

Go and open the door,
There might be a football player on a pitch,
Maybe there's a dinosaur as big as a mountain troll.

Go and open the door,
Then if there's nothing there, at least you'll be cool.

Matthew Barrow (8)
Dosthill Primary School

The Door

(Based on 'The Door' by Miroslav Holub)

Go and open the door
Maybe outside there's a pool, deep like the ocean shore.

Go and open the door
Maybe there's a ski ramp, slippery like the wet floor.

Go and open the door
Maybe there's a car, fast like a twister.

Go and open the door
Maybe there's $100, green like the grass.

Go and open the door
Maybe there's a chocolate egg, big like a bin.

Kieran Murden (9)
Dosthill Primary School

Quickly

Quickly the teacher runs down the hall
Quickly the children kick the ball
Quickly the teacher teaches the class
Quickly the children run on the grass.

Quickly the old man catches the ball
Quickly the Greeks run with a map
Quickly the man runs with a cat
Quickly the headmaster runs back saying, 'You can't do that.'

Jack Mason (8)
Dosthill Primary School

The Door

(Based on 'The Door' by Miroslav Holub)

Go and open the door
Maybe inside there's lava, red as cats' eyes,
Or an elephant with big ears.
Go and open the door,
Maybe you'll hear bugs crawling about
And nibbling on scraps.
Go and open the door,
You will be able to see what is there,
Or you could see a giant.

Anthony Johnston (8)
Dosthill Primary School

Quickly

Quickly lightning strikes an electric wire
Quickly the old man lights up his fire.

Quickly Trevor bends his bike wheels
Quickly the little ant smells and feels.

Quickly the funny man falls off the bus
Quickly the policeman makes a big fuss.

Quickly Frank jumps off the cliff
He can't climb back up so he often takes the lift.

Harry Cross (8)
Dosthill Primary School

The Door

(Based on 'The Door' by Miroslav Holub)

Go and open the door
Maybe there's a mansion gigantic like a giant.

Go and open the door,
Maybe there's the biggest swimming pool
Big like the biggest garden.
Maybe there's famous people
Singing like they're at a disco.

Go and open the door,
Maybe there's animals you love,
Like big horses.
Maybe there's chocolate city,
Big like London.

Go and open the door,
Even if the sun's shining,
Even if the stars are bright,
Even if there's the moon.

Go and open the door,
At least there will be some kind of light.

Georgina Holyland (8)
Dosthill Primary School

The Door

(Based on 'The Door' by Miroslav Holub)

Go and open the door
Maybe there's a Concorde like the whizzing air
Go and open the door
Maybe there's a dinner as lovely as chocolate
Go and open the door
Maybe there's a rock as hard as a brick
Go and open the door
Maybe there's a rocket launcher as quick as a Lamborghini.

Harry Tallis (9)
Dosthill Primary School

My Cat Cyril

My cat Cyril loves to dribble on my bedroom floor
My cat Cyril loves to attack
He sticks his claw in my mat
When he's happy he's a funny little chappy.

When he's hungry I give him food
But then he isn't in the mood
If you open tins, then put them in the bin
Cyril will come down and pull a little frown.

Rosie Espley (10)
Doxey Primary School

My Fish

Yo my fish is gold,
But he is so bold
He is so funny
He looks like a bunny
His eyes are so black
He's scared of cats
He loves food
But he's in a mood.

Dean Wheatley (10)
Doxey Primary School

Football

Football is such fun,
Playing in the sun.
I always get mucky,
But I am not very lucky.
When I play,
I always kick it out of the way.

Matthew Milsom (9)
Doxey Primary School

Football

I like playing footy
On the street
With my friends,
We have lots of fun,
We kick the ball
At the wall,
We pop the ball,
Sometimes with a big bang!

Joshua Bell (9)
Doxey Primary School

Playing

Playing every day,
Even on a Sunday.
Never stop, got to play,
Always win on a Tuesday.
Playing tig on a Wednesday,
Never stop, got to run.
Time to go,
See you next day.

Luke O'Brien (10)
Doxey Primary School

The School

School, school, brilliant school,
We get to go in the swimming pool.
My friends treat me like a fool,
School, school, brilliant school.
Everybody thinks they are cool.
Every day they play pool.
School, school, brilliant school.

Sophie Redden (9)
Doxey Primary School

School, School, School

School is boring,
Hear me say,
I can't wait,
'Til I go out to play.

Here comes lessons,
Science, English, maths,
How interesting,
Ha! Don't make me laugh.

Lunchtime's here,
Teacher calls my name,
Ready to go and eat,
What a riot it became!

PE is here I must say,
I think netball's great,
Home time's next, hooray!
Now I'm gonna play with my mates.

Emily Máté (10)
Doxey Primary School

I Love To Swim

I love to swim,
And it's great to win.
When you're swimming in the pool,
The water is very, very cool.
If you sink,
Most people's cheeks go pink.
But if you think,
You won't sink.
I go every Thursday,
It's so much fun.

Rebecca Johnson (10)
Doxey Primary School

My Dog Blackie

My dog Blackie
He's got a friend called Mackie
My dog Blackie has got a girlfriend called Ria
My dog Blackie drinks a lot of beer.

My dog Blackie likes to sleep
My dog Blackie likes to creep
My dog Blackie nearly died
I'm her owner and I saved her life.

Jordan Farmer (9)
Doxey Primary School

Football

Football is great,
I play every day,
My friends play too,
We score goals every day,
We even play on Sundays,
In the mud and rain,
I really enjoy playing,
With my friend too.

Marc Webber (10)
Doxey Primary School

Boring

School is boring
PE is cool
History's naff
And rubbish is school
I'm always snoring
Because school's so boring!

David Daddo-Langlois (9)
Doxey Primary School

Football

I play football
For my good school
I play striker
It is such fun
I play football a lot
Even in the hot
I score goals
What a team we are
And we beat teams by far.

Joe Hardwick (10)
Doxey Primary School

My Cat

My cat is brown
He acts like a clown
I know he is very playful
Although he is not very careful
He is my best pal
And he wears a bell.

Edward Dalton (9)
Doxey Primary School

I'm Scared

I'm scared
My mum's scared
My dad's scared
My sister's scared
My brother's scared
Are you scared?

Kyle Milgate (9)
Doxey Primary School

Brilliant

He's brilliant at karate
He's brilliant at darts
He's brilliant at acting
He's gets the best parts.

He's brilliant at swimming
He's brilliant at skates
He's brilliant at juggling
With real china plates.

He's brilliant at poetry
He's brilliant at rhyme
He's brilliant at lessons
He comes top every time.

Ria Buckley (9)
Doxey Primary School

Joey Banana

Joey Banana is well cool
He thinks teachers are a drool
He always plays football with his mates
The game they play is kicking balls at crates
'Sport is fun,' he says
Playing on the sandy bays
Cricket, basketball, whatever he plays
Even trying to reach the sun's rays
He's a laze lying there in the maize
That's old Joey Banana.

Cathy Hardwick (10)
Doxey Primary School

My Little Puppy

My little puppy,
Sat on a mat,
Licking his paws,
What do you say about that?
He's always mucky,
Because he's never lucky.

Here comes another dog,
Playing outside,
Here comes a fight,
Then they're on the way,
Soon it will be May,
Because he likes to play in the sun,
It's so much fun!

Katie Tunnicliffe (9)
Doxey Primary School

Nessy The Dragon

I had a dragon called Nessy
Who was very messy
She had a friend called Frank
Who pulled a very big prank
And it soon went blank
Then Nessy went to sleep with Frank.

Stephen Chilton (10)
Doxey Primary School

Running

As I started to run that day
I thought it would be so fun
Then I found out, how far I had to run
I ran through every street
But I didn't stop for one big drink
Then I noticed the jumps ahead
They were way too high to jump
But I didn't stop for one big drink
The race went on through night and day
And I decided it wasn't much fun
But I didn't stop, didn't stop
Because I wanted to win so much
A year went by and I was now 10
I did stop for one big drink
I carried on and saw a ribbon
I knew I was nearly there
I didn't let anyone pass
I knew I was nearly there at last
Then I went past the finish line
'Hip hip hooray,' I said
I went on the chair with the trophy
I didn't know what to say
So I went to have a long drink
Oh what a day! More like a year
So there you have it, goodbye.

Charlotte Ford (9)
Doxey Primary School

My Family Poem

Mum's in the kitchen cooking my tea,
Dad's in the garage fixing my bike for me,
Lou's in her room, which is as neat as can be,
And as for Charlie, she's stuck up a tree!

Amy Thompson (10)
English Martyrs Catholic Primary School

A Limerick

There was a young girl from Leek
To find a young horse she would seek,
She sat on a mare,
Got thrown through the air,
And couldn't get up for a week!

Hannah George (11)
English Martyrs Catholic Primary School

The Wind

The wind runs through the night,
Sounding just like dynamite.

Howling,
Growling,
Screeching,
Crying,
Moaning,
Groaning,
Grumbling,
Rumbling,
Tumbling,
Drumming,
Humming,
Twirling,
Curling,
Crashing,
Smashing,

The wind runs through the night,
Sounding just like dynamite.

Tom Goodwin (11)
Faber RC Primary School

Holiday

Holidays are the greatest thing,
Even if the phone goes ring,
Me, Mum and Dad are never sad,
But my sisters are always bad,
Mum thought she'd seen a rat,
Then Dad saw a real big bat,
When we went shopping,
I was always hopping,
No TV for at least a week,
But still we climbed the highest peak,
We went to Venice,
Where we played tennis,
When we got back we played a board game,
Then the next night we did the same,
Every day we went to the pool,
Which I jumped in, to get cool,
It took us a long time just to get there,
But that did include a trip to the fair,
My sisters both went swimming,
At the arcade I was winning,
Sometimes I read my book,
While my sisters had to cook,
When I went fishing I caught a fish,
Then that night it was on my dish,
We went for a walk into the town,
Mum and Dad had put on a frown,
When we had got home,
We brought a new gnome.

Jacob Collier (10)
Faber RC Primary School

Brer Rabbit And Brer Turtle

Brer Rabbit and Brer Turtle
Had a race on day.
They decided to run
A very long way.

Out in the sunshine
Rabbit did lie.
He knew that he didn't
Even have to try.

He looked at all the colours
Of the birds and dragonflies
And then turned over
And closed his eyes.

He woke with a start
When a sparrow pecked his face.
'You'd better hurry up
If you're going to win the race.'

Rabbit got to the winning post
Only to find
That turtle had got there
And left him behind.

Turtle's family had
Helped him win the race
And he looked at Brer Rabbit
With a smile on his face.

Turtle said
'That's a bag of juicy lettuce you owe me.
Meet me here tomorrow
At quarter to three.'

Isaac Cooke (11)
Faber RC Primary School

Teachers!

Children and teachers don't get along,
The singing teacher well she's a song.
She always has a good beat,
Telling me to get to my seat.

The school janitor has hairy knees,
Always carrying huge bunches of keys.
Always poking us with his broom,
All he brings us is pain and gloom.

The science teacher well she's over the moon,
Always singing her happy tune.
Don't waste time we've got till noon,
Thank goodness I'm leaving soon.

The history teacher always like to mime,
Now I'm thinking he's back from time.
He is very old and grey,
He is like he is from the olden days.

The art teacher is good with paint,
Sometimes she would like to faint.
But many times she does not stop
And it looks like she is going to pop.

The headmaster is a tight fist,
Always doing a homework list.
He has his hair pulled back,
I would give him the sack!
. . . If I was able to.

Olivia Van Tienen (10)
Faber RC Primary School

A Poem About My Family

I love all my family,
They are the best,
Except for Christopher -
He's a pest!
My grandad is wrinkly,
His teeth are all gone,
His dog's name is Shelly,
He has only one.
My mum's really clever,
She's done a degree,
She wants to go teaching,
But not to teach me!
My dad likes computer games
And sleeping in the chair,
He's got a big tummy
And lots of grey hair.
Chris drives me crazy,
He sneaks in my room,
He plays 'Harry Potter'
And flies on Mum's broom.
Jack is my cousin,
He's noisy and cute,
He loves Thomas Tank Engine
And shouts out, 'Toot-toot.'
James is my favourite,
He's mad on DVDs,
His girlfriend's Amanda
And his garden's full of weeds!
To round it all off I'd just like to say
Thank you for all of them - hip hip hooray!

Rhiannon Gibson (9)
Faber RC Primary School

The Pied Piper

There was a town called Hamelin
And rats were a plague to the bin.
A pied piper came along to help
And drowned the rats in River Pelp.
He asked for his reward,
But the mayor was stern as a sword.
So that man thought up a plan
And all the children ran.
Did I say all?
Oh no, not all.
For one little child,
Who was so mild,
Did not go,
Oh no, oh no.

Naomi Tyers (9)
Faber RC Primary School

Cruising

Bacon and egg waiting for you,
Every morning that's certainly true,
Then off on a trip,
That's not a skip,
Then after your nap,
You give them a tip,
On the way back you see many sights
And also loads of different flights,
But you know the day's gone,
And it's really shone,
So come back next year,
To have another beer.

Harry Mellor (10)
Faber RC Primary School

A Poem Cornwall

C ornish ice cream is the best
O ur caravan was lovely
R hiannon and I swam in the sea
N ewquay is the best for surfing
W atching the seagulls eating chips
A nd Mackie digging holes on the beach
L icking lollies in the sun
L ands End was where we saw the wreck

R ock pools and catching crabs in a net
O ctopuses swimming in the sea
C akes in cafés for our tea
K icking footballs, playing badminton
S trawberry milkshake from McDonald's!

I can't *wait* to go back there again!

Christopher Gibson (7)
Faber RC Primary School

Lava Lamp

Me and my lava lamp have lots of fun,
You cannot get me away from him, he is just so great.

Lava is his name, well lava lamp to be exact,
A lava lamp is a . . . well . . . strange to put it that way.
Very good at being blobby though,
A strange little object in fact.

Like a little lump of lava
Alone sitting there just blobbing about.
My mum and dad think he is very interesting and amazing,
Pretty and popular is my lava lamp.

Nicola Sellers (10)
Faber RC Primary School

My Holiday In Spain

Playing on the beach
Making sandcastles
Oh no! In comes the tide!
And now my castle's died!

We go back to our villa
And get our costumes on
We have a little swim
And then we go in

We go to our rooms
And get changed
Mum says, 'We're having tea,
In Alicante!'

So we start walking
To the restaurant
We sit down to eat
Lots of salad and meat

We go back to the villa
It's now bedtime
I try to stay up late
But I'm only eight.

Elizabeth Thrush (9)
Faber RC Primary School

War

War is bad and very sad,
People are hurt and feel like dirt,
Men are fed their daily bread,
The same old food, cold and stale,
People die and aren't very merry,
Dreaming of home and warm sherry,
Shooting and being shot
'And that is the end,' said Mr Pot.

Nicholas Cooper (8)
Faber RC Primary School

My Holiday

A holiday in Cornwall
Is really quite a ball.
Playing in the sea
My family, friends and me,
Playing different games.
We shout each other's names,
Catch the ball
Please don't let it fall
Is the one we like to play.
At the end of the day
We would all like to say
Goodnight
Sleep tight
Hope the bugs
Don't bite!

Joe Clowes (8)
Faber RC Primary School

Rainy Days

I hate a rainy day
No time to have a little play
Rain, drip drop, drip drop
On my rooftop
It was a real downpour
It soaked all the floor

It was really damp
We didn't want to camp
The gutter was gushing
The people were rushing
It was really grey
It was a dull day.

Beth Hall (8)
Faber RC Primary School

Smudge

My dog is called Smudge.
She eats lots of fudge.
When I say, 'Come here,'
She will disappear.
When she goes out to play
She likes to jump in the hay.
She chews on Mum's cardigan
And roots in her garden.
Then Mum gets cross,
Smudge knows she is the boss.
The milkman is her mate,
She hopes he won't be late
Because when he comes
There are always biscuits for her tum.

Sam Phillips (8)
Faber RC Primary School

My Horse And I

My horse and I jump
as high as the sky.
My horse and I gallop
as fast as the wind.

We are free to go wherever we want.
My horse and I are best friends
and will stay together to the end.
My horse and I.

Harriet Ferns (7)
Faber RC Primary School

My Dog Harvey

Harvey is my dog,
I love him a lot.
I love it when he's funny,
He really makes me laugh.
I like to throw him sticks
He loves to chew them.
He fights with Elmo
My other dog.
He doesn't mind my cats.
He like to moan,
But he only wants his food.
We got him from the kennels
When he was just a pup.
He was only three months old
And now he is four years old.
I love little Harvey
Although he can be a pest.
He drives my dad up the wall
Even if he's not in the car.
He's very sweet of course.

Jack Walker-Clarke (9)
Faber RC Primary School

My Dad's Boat

The boat chugged along the river,
The sun reflected on the bank
My arms gave a shiver
And my legs were all a quiver
The planks were cold,
I was told to stay on the boat.
The boat chugged along the river.

The people on the towpath waved,
We waved back,
Then it started to rain,
We put on our waterproof macs.

Abigale Salter (8)
Faber RC Primary School

What Am I?

I am black and like to fly,
I am scared when people want to touch me,
I am oval shaped and I like to hurt people,
I am very scared,
So if you try to creep, you will still scare me,
I don't have much family,
I am not very playful and I hate bouncing
What am I?

Emma-Louise Watton (7)
Flash Ley Primary School

Monday's Dog

Monday's dog takes my toast,
Tuesday's dog chews the post,
Wednesday's dog bites my leg,
Thursday's dog learns to beg,
Friday's dog eats my chicken,
Saturday's dog is good at licking,
But the dog that' s born on the Sabbath day
Is all of them and more OK!

Helena Fazackerley (9)
Flash Ley Primary School

Haiku Poem - Waves

Crash the bay today
I love waves on the beach now
Watch them bashing sand.

Tristan Veasey (8)
Flash Ley Primary School

An Evil Spell To Make Parents Disappear

Round about the cauldron go,
In these hideous objects throw,
Two bats, grime and an elephant's toenail,
Snot, books and a little quail.
Mix it up, make it slimy,
In go sixteen thousand cockroaches, just watch
them wriggle.
Camel's head watch it dribble,
Slugs and snails, centipedes and millipedes,
Big ones, small ones, giant ones,
Camel spit, human's hand and a pig's head,
A load of snail guts resting on a soil bed,
A bloody sword it looks like mouldy jam
And some skulls in a big cram,
Some fish eyes, and a good old kick, rinsed down
with a cup of sour pig sick.

Thomas Powell (10)
Flash Ley Primary School

Bonfire Night

The great big crimson, yellow and
Orange beast blazing in the background,
Fireworks crackling in the dark, starry
Sky like willow trees swaying in the night.
Bangs like drums fade away,
The howling and barking of dogs that have been tied up,
The smell of smoke settling in the air,
Children shouting and running about,
All the smells of chestnuts and potatoes,
Sparklers being written with in the sky,
The crackling of wood in the amazing fire,
Guy Fawkes tied to a stick above the fire
Slowly burning away.

Cathryn Evans (10)
Flash Ley Primary School

Monday's Dog

Monday's dog stood on his knees,
Tuesday's dog had Chinese,
Wednesday's dog goes all fluffy,
Thursday's dog is all scruffy,
Friday's dog howls in the night,
Saturday's dog gives you a fright,
And the dog that was born on the Sabbath Day
We give him a bone in May.

Bethany Cresswell (8)
Flash Ley Primary School

Monday's Dog

Monday's dog chases his tail,
Tuesday's dog eats a snail,
Wednesday's dog is so fluffy,
Thursday's dog is so scruffy,
Friday's dog has the roasts,
Saturday's dog eats the post,
And the dog that was born on the seventh day,
Eats the birds every May.

Joshua Ratcliffe (9)
Flash Ley Primary School

Monday's Dog

Monday's dog is much too fat,
Tuesday's dog is afraid of a cat,
Wednesday's dog walks all the way to play,
Thursday's dog sleeps through the day,
Friday's dog has a very loud bark,
Saturday's dog can play in the park,
And the dog that was born on the Sabbath day
Is cheerful and always likes to play.

Adrian Wood (9)
Flash Ley Primary School

An Evil Spell

Guts and blood mixed in,
A pig's tail with seven snails,
Some contents out of a bin,
Cows' sick floating and flowing,
Dirty toenails swishing and swirling,
Ugly bugs bobbing up and down,
Then throw in two fish eyes looking
Straight at you,
After a piece of snot sailing to the bottom,
Some human spots sinking down and down,
Human skin staying at the top,
Sheep guts all covered in blood,
Then in goes some yellow earwax,
That smells out the room,
Then last of all the human head.

Ross Newell (10)
Flash Ley Primary School

The Evil Spell

Wet troll bogies all mixed in,
With slimy blood and human skin
Cod fish eyes and slimy snails
Dragon's vomit and fingernails,
Bat fur covered in sparrow's dribble,
All mixed up in rotten scribble,
Take all this and you will find,
The teacher's gone away to hide,
Stir and turn the cauldron round
Puff! The teacher's gone underground,
Crash! He's gone to the Devil's lair,
There's no children at all down there.

Emma Price (10)
Flash Ley Primary School

An Evil Spell

Guts and blood mixed in together,
With slugs and roaches saved forever,
Put in voodoo with two arms, legs with
Cow sick and rusty pegs.
Double, double, toil and trouble,
Fire burn and cauldron bubble,
Chuck some stick insects and more frogs,
With four small dead cats and dogs,
Mix this well and you will get your
Teacher gone and you can forget.

Luke Bufton (10)
Flash Ley Primary School

The Bonfire

Guy sitting on the top,
Raging flames that never stop,
The colour so bright,
I just couldn't stand the sight,
Banging here, banging there,
The firework so fast, it blew my hair!
Now Guy is burning even more,
On Bonfire Night that's the law!

Renae Phipps (11)
Flash Ley Primary School

A Noisy Day

Children chattering,
Rain pattering on the ground,
Babies crying,
With headaches from the sound.

Caroline Begley (11)
Flash Ley Primary School

A Good Spell To Make The World Peaceful

Round about the cauldron go,
In these wondrous objects throw
A shiny snowflake in it goes,
A happy song away it flows.
A golden wishing star watch it shoot by,
Some angel wings look at them fly,
Double, double happy world,
The world will be peaceful again.
Add a smell of a rose,
Then put in some nice red bows,
Put in glitter to make girls shine
An angel's halo to make things fine.
Double, double happy world,
A magic wand to cast the spell,
A happy heart to make things well,

The world will be peaceful again.

Emma Foster (10)
Flash Ley Primary School

An Evil Spell To Make My Teacher Mad

Round about the cauldron go,
In these hideous objects throw.
Frogs' legs mixed with rotten milk,
Carefully stirred with sheets of silk.
Take much care and get it right,
Stir and stir with all your might.
Horse manure to make it smell,
Old hags' noises hear them yell.
To make my teacher fret and fume,
I will use the potion that would pop a balloon.

Charlotte Thorpe (9)
Flash Ley Primary School

Bonfire Night

A fountain of colours explode in the sky,
Glittering like rubies, emeralds and pearls,
Then, like rain, down they fall.

The fiery beast's raging roars,
Its dancing flames cast shadows on walls,
And they wrap the guy, pulling him down.

Rockets cut through the heavens like spears,
Leaving a trail of scarlet behind them.

The sky is filled with colours once more,
But soon the excitement dies away,
'Cause the fiery beast breathes one last breath,
And the wisps of smoke which were once in the air,
Floated and disappeared . . .

Rebecca Li (11)
Flash Ley Primary School

A Magic World

Someone with a nose who likes to
Pose with a gorgeous nose,
Double, double fun and laughter,
I'll make good forever after,
One baby kitten with a little mitten
Out on the streets and he has been bitten,
Double, double fun and laughter,
I'll make good forever after.
My mum is sweet, she likes to pose
Holding onto a sweet red rose.

Jessica Young (10)
Flash Ley Primary School

My Poem

A rosy flower, a summer's day,
Sweets and candy, come your way.
A star above, a winter wish,
Double, double fun and laughter,
I'll make good for ever after,
My mom is sweet, she likes to pose
Holding a sweet red rose.

Sarah Sharp (10)
Flash Ley Primary School

In The Jungle

R ummaging through the leaves, the armadillo goes,
A ntennae's searching the anthills, for ants,
I nside, the forest quivers with silence,
N ow the forest is coming alive,
F rom all over animals are coming,
O n the floor the animals are scattering,
R acing around in all directions,
E verywhere the Indians roar, hunting their food, so beware!
S ilence now has overcome,
T he animals are settling for the night.

Michael Price (11)
Flash Ley Primary School

Dogs

Dogs
Dungeon dingos,
Dotty Dalmatians groomed,
Dancing dogs, discovering dangerously,
DJ dogs dance and disturb.

Billy Walker (11)
Flash Ley Primary School

Bonfires

Bonfires whirlpools, sucking Guy Fawkes in,
Rockets whistling, bang, crash, crackling,
Children writing their names with a dancing, prancing sparkler,
Fireworks, like fountains glistening in the moonlight,
Catherine wheels whirling cutting through the air,
People staring, watching with amazement,
Watching the stunning fireworks show!
Hear the children scream and shout when they
Watch the bonfire go out,
Now it's time to go home, the ash from the fire left all alone.

Molly-Ann Luckman (10)
Flash Ley Primary School

Moses And The Burning Bush

I didn't know what was happening,
All I saw was this burning bush appear,
I heard Lord God calling 'Moses, Moses,'
I felt like I was in a weird dream,
He kept talking to me and told me to
Go and save his people,
I covered my eyes in disbelief,
'Believe me,' God said, 'I will help you all the way.'

Jack Ward (11)
Flash Ley Primary School

The Stars (Haiku)

Bright in the night's sky,
Lighting up the black background,
Silently twinkling.

Leigh Banner (11)
Flash Ley Primary School

The Best Match

Ping of the post
Shriek of the whistle
Shuffle of feet
Splash of mud
Clash of bodies
Thump of the ball
Roar of the crowd
It was the best game of all.

Jordan Bloor (11)
Flash Ley Primary School

Bonfire Night

Bonfire Night is there to enjoy,
Bombs exploding everywhere,
Children screaming and shouting loudly,
Colours scattering in different shapes,
Crackling sounds way up in the sky,
Whistling sounds all around,
Sparks sprinkling on the ground.

Emily Boulton (11)
Flash Ley Primary School

Kangaroo

Jumping,
Bouncing about,
Crunching the sweet dewed grass,
Jumping around with a joey,
Boxing.

Sarah Till (11)
Flash Ley Primary School

Bonfire Night

Crackle, crackle, crackle goes the fire,
With its beautiful reds, oranges and yellows,
Old Guy Fawkes on top staring down,
Looking sad and all alone.

Boom, boom, boom go the fireworks,
All coloured fountains in the air
Some scattering some just flying,
A couple twinkle like stars at night.

Ha, ha, ha go the people in excitement,
Looking up in the sky with astonishment,
Talking about the beautiful colours in the sky,
While babies cry at the sound of the boom.

While you enjoy it you best watch out,
The danger of fire burning you,
Imagine getting hit with a firework,
So keep safe and enjoy.

Mary-Ann Wilson (11)
Flash Ley Primary School

The Cheetah

Meat eater,
Bone cruncher,
Neck biter,
Zebra catcher,
Wildebeest killer,
Wild prowler,
Morning hunter,
Death bringer,
Fast runner,
Warthog slayer,
Fierce growler.

Roxanne Buckley (10)
Flash Ley Primary School

Moses And The Burning Bush

As I heard the crackle of the fire and
The lambs bleat,
I was scared of the Holy God,
I asked Him, 'Why me?'
With the soft, warm ground under my feet
I began to pray,
The taste and smell of smoke and fire,
I crept away at His final words.

Rebecca Bright (11)
Flash Ley Primary School

Who Am I?

I am long, thin, wooden, strong,
Hard and powerful,
Sometimes I am snapped,
I am brown and black,
I am big and I am pretty ugly,
I hit a ball and I play a game.

Ryan Keay (7)
Flash Ley Primary School

What Am I?

I am shaped like a circle,
I go in the sky,
I am white and shiny,
Everyone sees me in the sky,
I shine through your window,
Can you guess what I am?

Bradley Ecclestone (8)
Flash Ley Primary School

It's A Beautiful Day

It's a beautiful day,
No clouds beside me,
It's a beautiful day,
Touch me,
Take me to the open place,
Take me to the open road.

We are just at the end of the rainbow,
It's an excellent day,
The sun is shining with a great beam,
It's a beautiful day,
It's snowing beautifully,
It's an excellent day.

Ben Hildred (10)
Greenacres CP School

Once Upon A Rhyme

Once upon a time,
In a nursery rhyme,
The trees singing everywhere,
There's even a bear singing over there.

There's a pen,
Writing with some men,
There's even a pan,
Cooking with a man.

So come to the rhyme land,
It's only the same as the sand.

Daniel Mills (11)
Greenacres CP School

Snow

It's snowing today,
Why don't we go and play?
The snow was nice,
It turned into ice.

It's snowing today,
I can see footprints about,
It falls from the sky,
It's ever so high.

It's snowing today,
I can see the icicles,
The children are playing around,
There's snow on the ground,
It's snowing today.

Jade Moore (11)
Greenacres CP School

Winter Wonderland

Snow is crunchy,
Snow is cold,
Snow is like a white blanket,
Snow is blobby,
When it snows, I feel happy,
When the snow has gone, I feel down.

When the snow is here, you can see
Things that are here when you are not here.

Snowballs flying,
Teachers crying,
Children ducking,
Snowball playtime!

Craig Westbrook (11)
Greenacres CP School

Winter, Winter

Winter, winter it can be fun,
When it is snowy you can't run,
When it snows, I have marshmallows,
When I have them, I see cold windows.

Coldy, coldy when I cross,
I will Jack Frost,
It will be so snowy tonight,
Could it be so bright?

Snow, snow will it be freezing?
But my friends will be ice skating,
Weekends I go out with a Flake,
Is it a mistake?

Throwing, throwing could it hit anyone?
Where is everyone today?
There is a really long flow,
But where is the snow?

Jonathan Ricketts (10)
Greenacres CP School

Winter

Winter, winter
I love it when it snows,
If it don't I'm so low.

If it rains,
It confuses my brain.

When it is sunny,
Ice lollies are yummy.

When it is cloudy,
My mum says howdy.

Daniel Hicks (11)
Greenacres CP School

Snow, Winter, Snow

Snow, snow such a magical thing,
Drops down gently like a ring,
It comes down like a dream,
While it gleams through the sun,
While I dance, I run around,
I see birds sleep and sound,
When it goes, I'm bound to be sad,
But at least our pets will be glad.

Winter, winter gives you chills,
Good idea to ride the hills,
Every time it is winter,
I wait until my cat's had its litter,
It is beautiful when the birds come out to play,
But it's the next day and I can't wait until the next winter.

Snow, snow pouring down,
If it doesn't I will frown,
More and more I smile,
Snow, snow I like your style
When it goes, I am sad,
But oh well, I am glad.

Sarah Averne (11)
Greenacres CP School

The Snow

As the snow glistened in the morning light,
I saw the tiny footprints of a bird,
The snow makes a white cover over the world,
It's as if there's just me in the whole wide world,
As the snow flutters from the misty sky,
A secret is hidden beneath the snow,
The snow drips down from the trees so high,
I wonder, I wonder what secrets are hidden
Beneath the snow, who knows?

Kayleigh Price (10)
Greenacres CP School

Snow Time

Teacher's coming, what shall we do?
I know I'll throw a snowball at you.

Snowballs,
Snowmen.

Head's coming I know what I'll do,
I think I'll throw a snowball at you.

Teacher's bawling,
Children crawling.

Snowballs,
Snowmen,
Snow time!

Adam Alexander Lawson (10)
Greenacres CP School

The Beach

The beach is warm,
The beach is cool,
The beach has always been the same.

The sea is cold,
The sea is fun,
The sea has always been the same.

The shells feel fine,
The shells feel warm,
The shells have always been the same.

The sun is hot,
The sun is bright,
The sun has always been the same.

Danielle Ricketts (10)
Greenacres CP School

Real Madrid

Real Madrid scoring lots
Beckham to Ronaldo,
And he scores,
1-0 Beckham has a free kick
And it is 2-0
This game is unbelievable.

They come out for the second half,
There is 20 minutes to go,
Beckham has got another free kick,
It is 3-0
Now there is 15 minutes to go,
Zidane shoots, he scores
4-0
Full-time and Real Madrid have won
And they have won.

Matthew Averne (11)
Greenacres CP School

It's Bedtime With A Rhyme

Little Red Riding Hood,
Went into the wood,
She went to see her grandma
And did all she could
Out came her grandpa
And bit off her head and then
They found that she was dead.

Cinderella covered in yellow
Went downstairs to meet a fellow
She met a man and said 'Hello'
And the man said, 'Oh no.'

Holli Edwards (10)
Greenacres CP School

The Teachers!

At Greenacres the teachers are mad,
They tell you off if you are really bad,
Sometimes they confuse me,
Sometimes they're weird,
And by all the children, they're really feared.

Sometimes they can be fun in DT
And sometimes they can put you down in PE
Sometimes they can be sweet as a lemon and lime,
But unfortunately not most of the time.

Now I have set an example,
And it's time for you to take a sample,
Of the terrible teachers at Greenacres School.

Jack Stevenson-Smith (10)
Greenacres CP School

Miss Riding Hood

Little Red Riding Hood walked along
Singing a very jolly song,
Then who popped out the tree,
Mr Wolf skipping with glee.

They made their way to Grandma's house,
All they could hear was a little mouse,
When they opened the door,
Grandma was dead on the floor.

The murder weapon was discovered
And then the truth was uncovered,
Miss Riding Hood was found guilty,
And Mr Wolf skipped with glee.

Connah Roe (11)
Greenacres CP School

The Meeting Of Fairy Tales

Once there was a meeting,
A giant, giant meeting,
Of fairy tale characters,
Sending happy greetings.

The big bad wolf and the BFG,
Went and had a cup of tea,
Cinderella and Princess Belle,
Met the Devil who came from Hell.

The three little pigs and the three Billy goats,
Went to the shop and brought some coats,
Little Red Riding Hood, Shrek and Donkey,
Were shouting themselves really wonky.

The seven little dwarves and the three big bears,
Went to the salon and cut their hairs,
This party is weird, this party is mad,
This party's been fun, or at least it had.

Jonathan Poulton (10)
Greenacres CP School

The Wolf's Adventure

Little Red Riding Hood
Went into the wood
Off came her head,
She was dead
'Oops!' said the wolf.

He went into the pig's house,
They were sneaky, quiet as a mouse,
Then jumped out -
The wolf gave a shout
And was never heard of again.

Aimee Lunt (11)
Greenacres CP School

Fairy Tales

Peter Pan and Wendy
Flew up in the sky,
Tinkerbell flew after them
And soon passed by.

Little Red Riding Hood
Ran into the wood
Wolf ran after her
But landed with a thud.

Sleeping Beauty
Loves her sleep
She does it night and day
But when the prince wakes her up
She shouts 'Hooray!'

Sophie Critchlow (11)
Greenacres CP School

Snow In The City

Snow in the city,
It looks so pretty,
Like a white hand,
Covering the land.

Snow in the country,
It looks so crunchy,
It turns the grass to white,
All through the night.

Snow on the hills,
It gives you the chills,
Like ice cream on your teeth,
Creating a snowy, white wreath.

Tom Westwood (10)
Greenacres CP School

Pig And Wolf Mix Up

The three little pigs,
Wore three little wigs,
They were putting on a show,
It was about Christmas and snow.

When it had finished, the wolf
Went backstage,
He tried to catch them in a cage.

The pigs caught the wolf
And tied him with a rope,
He was praying to God
With all he could hope.

They took the wolf
Back to their home
On the way he kicked a gnome.

They chopped the wolf up
And left him for dead,
For supper they ate
Him with jam and bread.

Scott Heard (11)
Greenacres CP School

Fairy Tales Backwards

Three pigs saw the wolf in his house
By the curtain like a little mouse,
They blew it down and said it was the rain
Then the wolf went into hiding again.

Then there was Muffet sitting on a log,
Eating her pie and down came a frog,
So Miss Muffet ate away
That frog lasted her all day.

Ryan Matthews (11)
Greenacres CP School

It's Time For A Rhyme

Red Riding Hood went to bed,
The wolf came up,
And bit off her head,
Then Red Riding Hood was dead!

Cinderella was informed,
That Sleeping Beauty was bored,
She jumped off her chair,
Off went her hair,
Cinderella was eaten by a bear.

Mickey Mouse
Had a house,
At the bottom
Of the garden!

Nicola Leigh Wilcox (11)
Greenacres CP School

The Vampire In Wales

I know a vampire who lives in Wales,
He likes to eat slugs and snails.
If you get him in a mood,
He'll turn you into food.
But all the same, he likes me,
He drinks blood and serves me tea.
He goes for a curry every day,
And always scares the waiter away.
So if you ever come to stay,
Make sure you stay out of his way!

James Chapman (10)
Greenacres CP School

Little Red Riding Hood

Once upon a rhyme,
Miss Riding Hood
Went to see her granny,
Who lived in the wood.

A wolf came along,
And asked her where she was going,
She said, 'Up in the hills,'
Where it was snowing.

The wolf went up
And froze to death,
As little Red Riding Hood
Held her breath.

Miss Riding Hood's granny,
Was feeling ill,
But she was glad,
The wolf had died on the hill.

Little Red Riding Hood
Then lived in peace,
Until along came
The wolf's evil niece!

Hannah Welsh (11)
Greenacres CP School

Fairy Tale

The prince is such a fright,
Sully likes to fly a kite,
The Beast likes to take a flight,
And Dumbo is such a sight.

All over the place Pinocchio lies,
Peter Pan's fairy almost dies,
Little Jack Horner likes his pies,
And Aladdin's magic carpet flies!

Sophie Hinder (10)
Greenacres CP School

Fairy Tale Rhyme

In her bed Snow White dies,
Up in the air Peter Pan flies,
Oh her tuffet Miss Tuffet cries
And in a house Pinocchio lies.

In his castle, the beast is scary,
The wolf who catches the pigs are hairy,
Tinkerbell is Peter Pan's fairy,
The little lamb belongs to Mary.

Here is my fairy tale rhyme!
To be enjoyed at any time!

Hannah Fortune (10)
Greenacres CP School

Wondering What To Do

I'm sitting on a table thinking of a stable,
Wondering what to do.

I want my mom so I suck my thumb,
Wondering what to do.

There's a monkey in my room watching a cartoon,
Wondering what to do.

I am quite lazy, my mom's going crazy,
Wondering what to do.

There's a baboon holding a balloon ,
Wondering what to do.

There's a pear in a chair and it's growing hair,
Wondering what to do.

I'm sitting on a chair twiddling with my hair,
Wondering what to do.

Paige Savage (11)
Mary Howard Primary School

Outside Stood A Snowman

Outside stood a snowman,
Who had a carrot as a nose,
Outside stood a snowman,
Who was holding a water hose.
Outside stood a snowman
Who had buttons as a mouth,
Outside stood a snowman,
Who was facing south.
Outside stood a snowman,
Who had a purple hat,
Outside stood a snowman,
Who was cuddling my cat.
Outside stood a snowman
Who had buttons on his top,
Outside stood a snowman,
Who was about to flop.
Outside stood a snowman,
Who was by my side,
Outside stood a snowman,
Who just sadly died.

Mina Mahmoudzadeh (10)
Mary Howard Primary School

Dragon

Tiny tail
Little nails
And . . .
His wings become stronger
His teeth become longer.

Sophie Bagworth (7)
Mary Howard Primary School

War

Swords clashing,
Catapults bashing,
Arrows flying,
People dying,
Men falling,
Orcs mauling,
Cave trolls pushing,
Arrows whooshing,
Walls demolished,
Bows well polished,
Orcs dying,
Women crying,
Innocents dying,
Nazguls flying,
Cave trolls banging,
Drums clanging,
The war is over,
No more dying,
No more crying,
The war is over.

William Carter (11)
Mary Howard Primary School

Stood Outside

I'm stood outside,
A snowman melting,
People watching,
As I melt away more and more.
Crying people watch me dying!
As I feel my life is going
The snow began to melt as
I was shrinking fast,
I know that my life was
Over at last.

Jordan Broadhurst (11)
Mary Howard Primary School

The Lord Of The Rings

Gimli is smoking,
Aragorn is choking,
Gandalf is croaking.

Nazguls are flying,
Orcs are dying.

Faramir is running,
Treebeard is turning,
Bilbo is learning.

Pippin is trying,
Merry is crying,
While Sam is cooking.

Gollum is sneaking,
Frodo keeps seeking.

Bells ring,
Aragorn is king.

Richard Sammons (10)
Mary Howard Primary School

Snow

White stuff starts to fall,
Now we cannot play ball,
It's snow!
And for once it's putting on a show,
Yes! Yes! We can make a snowman at last,
Oh why do I have to have my leg in a cast?

People sliding down the hill
There's my best friend, Bill,
Bill's in a snowball fight,
The snow's brilliant white,
The snow fills us with joy!

Georgina Randall (10)
Mary Howard Primary School

The Lost Girl!

The girl stood cold and sad,
The girl is always bad!

The girl hovered on a string,
The girl had absolutely nothing!

The girl wept - all alone,
Her skin just covered her bones!

The girl had clothes like cardboard,
She felt like hardboard!

The girl had black mascara tears,
The girl's name was Leah!

The girl was very weird,
The girl had disappeared!

Scarlett Dixon (10)
Mary Howard Primary School

Lord Of The Rings

Oliphants dying,
Nazguls flying.

Orcs climbing,
Gondor men fighting.

Legolas firing,
Orcs falling.

Lord Aragorn slashing,
Cave trolls bashing.

Gondor men dashing,
Gate smashing.

Mount Doom crashing,
Gold ring flashing.

Harry Thomas (9)
Mary Howard Primary School

The Strange English Lesson

English, everyone hates,
Because we have Mr Baits,
Such a mardy teacher,
And a Sunday preacher.

Always doing a private talk,
And he has a silly walk,
We all make fun of him,
And we call him Mr Slim!

But this lesson was exceptionally strange,
Because we had a teacher change,
So we spent the afternoon,
Making up a stupid tune!

Now we have Mr Lame,
Who tells us stories of fame,
He's more boring than Mr Baits,
Who the class no longer hates.

Samantha Lucy Rose (10)
Mary Howard Primary School

Sledging

Yesterday, I went sledging with my brother,
We went down the safe slope,
Watched my mother,
Then onto the big slope,
It was such fun,
Racing with my brother,
Look at me,
I've won.

Alex Preece (8)
Mary Howard Primary School

Outside And Inside

The leaves were falling from the trees,
And I saw some bullying bees.

The rain trickled on my bright blue umbrella,
So I quickly ran down to my cellar.

I was jumping up and down,
And my mate was acting like a clown.

I was waiting for my tea and my brother
Was looking at me.

I felt very proud until I saw a big grey cloud.

I went down to my den and I saw a big fat hen!

I tried to get the hen out, it was eating my sprouts.

I went to bed and I bumped my head,
After that I thought I was dead!

David Chambers (9)
Mary Howard Primary School

The Blizzard That Blew Me Away

I went to play in the snow today,
A blizzard came and blew me away,
It went through the village and into the town,
Then it went around
And it stopped,
When the snow went plop,
On the ground.

Harry Martin (7)
Mary Howard Primary School

Demons

Swirling, swerving, twirling round
That's the sky demon above the ground,
Flash, flash, flash, flash, crack, crack,
The fire demon emerging from the black,
Rumble, rumble, rumble, dig, dig, dig,
The Earth demon is very, very big,
Bubble, bubble, bubble, froth, froth, froth,
The water demon never has to cough,
The moon demon flies to the moon,
On his brightly decorated balloon,
Flying, flying, flying, roaring, roaring,
That's the wind demon blowing,
Crack, crack, crack, hard, hard, hard,
The rock demon is the demon guard,
Bang, bang, bang, cold, cold, cold,
The metal demon is very bold.

Stephen Purkess (8)
Mary Howard Primary School

The Winter Shoot

One day I had to wake up late,
Then we went to the lake,
Then we got in the car,
And we went very far,
We went to the hut,
And got a cut,
Then we shot a duck,
And it was very good luck.
I ate it for lunch,
Then my brother gave me a punch.

Adam Rowe (7)
Mary Howard Primary School

My Favourite Seasons

Winter
People outside doing up their zip,
Ducks on the ice ready to slip,
Throwing snowballs is great fun,
No one outside daring to run.
Twenty snowmen standing outside,
Boys and girls having a slide,
No birds to have a race,
Strong wind blowing in my face.

Summer
The sun outside always will shine,
People outside drinking white wine,
Standing and talking in a queue,
Waiting for food from the barbecue,
We don't have school so that's very good,
There's another great thing, we won't have a flood,
Summer is my best season,
Birthday presents is my reason.

Spring
In spring leaves will grow,
All the gardeners will be getting out their hoes,
The blue sky is bright,
To fill me with delight,
All through spring,
The birds will sing,
The flowers will bloom,
To take away the gloom.

Pavan Dhillon (8)
Mary Howard Primary School

All About Egyptians

Egyptians are buried in tombs
For which they have left us clues
They were put in coffins.
First went the king
Then went the slaves
And that was the end.
Archaeologists found the clues.

Lauren Simmons (9)
Moorgate Primary School

Dragons

A big thing, has deep and fiery breath,
A dragon has one big tail, two wings, one head,
Two legs and two arms.
Dragons cause chaos because of their fiery breath,
And set things on fire like plants, trees and homes.
But there's a way just to stop the creature,
That is to put water in its mouth.

Jake Barber (8)
Moorgate Primary School

Winter At Christmas Time

The colour of the snow glistening as white clouds,
With the wind whistling,
With every fluffy cloud floating by,
In a sleigh with sparkling skies,
Singing and laughing, hee, hee, hee!

Heber Robertson (8)
Moorgate Primary School

Teacher's Desk

T eacher's book (old)
E lephant rubber (worn out)
A lan's homework (in the bin)
C ameron's water (mouldy)
H anna's coffee (black)
E lla's pen (broken)
R on's elementary (rubbish)
S onia's vase (on the floor)

D eclan's book (torn)
E mily's maths (under the drawer)
S am's model (on Miss' chair)
K im's sharpener (in the drawer).

Molly Cotton (9)
Moorgate Primary School

Silver

S hiny as a star
I n the twinkling sky
L ovely light, brighter than my eye
V alentine in the silver rings
E ndless shimmering shine
R eaching round the world.

Laura Bennett (8)
Moorgate Primary School

Wonderful Winter

Crunchy frost bites your cold ears.
Wild, freezing snowballs thrusting madly through the air.
Like warm woolly jumpers, the snow covers the grass.
The cold winter air is wonderful.
Now let's go in for burnt buttery toast and delicious sugary tea!

Joseph Fowler (8)
Moorgate Primary School

Ice Cream

I ce cream comes in every flavour.
C reamy tastes, scrumptious!
E xtra chocolate, please!

C runchy cones and flakes.
R aspberry ripple is my favourite.
E at them now before they go.
A t the market they are sold.
M int chocolate, here I come!

Ross Orchard (8)
Moorgate Primary School

Silver

S hiny as a spoon
I nviting my reflection
L isten to the sound of the spoon tinkling
V ery impressive in a wooden drawer
E very day the silver sparkles
R eflecting through the world.

Charlie Brookes (8)
Moorgate Primary School

Football

The colour of the gleaming golden cup.
The sweet taste of victory.
The sound of the jeering crowd.
The beautiful sight of the Mexican wave.
The smell of half-time pie.
The feeling of the ecstatic crowd.

Matthew Nield (9)
Moorgate Primary School

Blue

Blue is the colour of the sky
Blue is the colour of a dye
Blue is the colour of the lake
Blue is the colour of the iced cake
Blue is the colour of the cup
Blue is the colour of the book
Blue is the colour of the rain
Blue is the colour of fizzing pop that stained
Blue is the colour of the fish
Blue is the colour of the dish.

But the colour blue is not me!

Declan Hartwell (9)
Moorgate Primary School

Summer

S trange glowing beams shining in the field
U nder the trees there are beautiful green leaves
M other always looks after the children
M ean people being nice
E nding of the world coming to the beginning of the world
R ed and tanned people wandering around the garden.

Ben Wright (8)
Moorgate Primary School

Dragon

The fierce dragon flies through the black shiny sky,
With flames coming out of the frightful dragon's snout.
Its elegant wings flap gracefully while in flight,
It lives in a smoky volcano and blasts fire to cook his leg mutton.

Sam Taylor (9)
Moorgate Primary School

Your Clue To Summer Feelings

Summer is bright and blue.
You can hear many people, this is very true.
The sun is light
And it's a good time to fly a kite.
It feels like I'm in an oven
But I'm on the beach and I'm in Heaven.
Summer is bright and blue.
This is your only clue.

Reese Boulton (9)
Moorgate Primary School

Shiny Silver

The shiny silver of light
What a lovely sight
It sparkles in the moonlight
The darkness bows to the shining light
It glitters on a car of white
A silver crane that has such height
It is such a lovely sight.

Jack Watson (9)
Moorgate Primary School

The Good Memories Of My Best Friend Brandy

His golden fur and gleaming eyes.
The taste of happiness.
He ran so fast his ears appeared to fly.
The sight of his play.
The smell of fur was in the air.
He will be my best friend forever from today.

Paul Eglinton (8)
Moorgate Primary School

The Ancient Egyptians

A mazing people known for building pyramids
N ear our world, they
C reated
I ntelligence
E ven
N ow
T hey tell of

E gypt by
G iving clues.
Y oung
P eople
T alk
I n
A
N ew
S peech.

Megan Webster (9)
Moorgate Primary School

Hidden Thoughts

H oping your secrets will not flee
I nflexible mind
D etermined to keep your thoughts
D eceive to protect your secrets
E steem your thoughts
N ever tell anyone.

T rying and trying not to tell a word
H urt mind and soul trying to keep them in
O beying your secrets
U nderstanding that you must never tell
G esture to people
H esitate over saying anything
T aking your secrets and mind apart
S o please don't say I have secrets!

Hannah Carver (9)
Moorgate Primary School

Egyptians

E gypt is very interesting
G iving clues
Y oung
P eople
T ravel
I nside
A ncient pyramids.
N owhere else do they
S tand in our world.

Tom Clarke (8)
Moorgate Primary School

The Silver Moon

The silver moon comes out at night,
The silver moon shines so bright.
It makes the night look like day,
I really do like it that way.
Now the sun is in the sky,
And the silver moon says, 'Goodbye.'

Charlotte Swarbrick (8)
Moorgate Primary School

Ice Cream

Scrumptious
    tasty
        mouth-watering
melting in the summer sun.

Abbi Rose Bartlett (8)
Moorgate Primary School

Blue

Blue is the colour of the sky
Blue is the colour of hair dye
Blue is the colour of the new wedding cake
Blue is the colour of the lake
Blue is the colour of the rain
Blue is the colour of even more rain
Now I feel blue too.

Josh Pointon (8)
Moorgate Primary School

Summer Feelings

Blue skies and white fluffy clouds,
Tasty fruit, creamy tea.
Children screaming, shouting, playing in the street,
Ice-cold Coke in the summer sun.
Feeling happy and playful,
Life is sunny and bright.

Katrina Williams (9)
Moorgate Primary School

Gleam

G lossy as a silver spoon
L ike the shiny moon.
E very night the dazzling stars come out
A cross the rippling river.
M oonlight shines over the black water.

Jack Clarke (7)
Moorgate Primary School

A Poem To Be Spoken Silently

It was so quiet that I heard
the wind blow through the draught of the window.

It was so quiet that I heard
someone's feet stamping on the soft ground of the classroom floor.

It was so quiet that I heard
the glue topple over on to the empty sheet of paper in the hot classroom.

It was so quiet that I heard
the silent water slide on to the quiet table.

It was so quiet that I heard
the bouncing globe crash down on to the soft carpet.

It was so quiet that I heard
the teacher lock the solid brown door.

Hannah Poole (8)
Our Lady & St Werburgh's RC Primary School, Newcastle-under-Lyme

A Poem To Be Spoken Silently

It was so quiet that I heard
someone biting their dirty fingernails.
It was so quiet that I heard
a robin fly with his wings flapping in the snowy air.
It was so quiet that I heard
a tortoise swimming across the warm ocean.
It was so quiet that I heard
some conkers fall on the concrete floor.
It was so quiet that I heard
the leaves swaying among the cold breeze.
It was so quiet that I heard
the sun rising among the clouds.

Harriet Rose Lowe (7)
Our Lady & St Werburgh's RC Primary School, Newcastle-under-Lyme

A Poem To Be Spoken Silently

It was so quiet that I heard
the watercolours slop on my empty page.

It was so quiet that I heard
the sunflowers grow in the frosty air.

It was so quiet that I heard
the wintry air twisting around our house.

It was so quiet that I heard
a big baby crawling on a wooden floor.

It was so quiet that I heard
the golden sun blaze in the blue sky.

It was so quiet that I heard
the teacher think her wonderful thoughts.

Abigail Hughes (8)
Our Lady & St Werburgh's RC Primary School, Newcastle-under-Lyme

A Poem To Be Spoken Silently

It was so quiet that I heard an enormous lamp post turn on.
It was so quiet that I heard some slimy toothpaste run on to the
prickly toothbrush.
It was so quiet that I heard a spiny book slam shut.
It was so quiet that I heard banging footsteps and a wicked laugh.
It was so quiet that I heard the round world slowly move.
It was so quiet that I heard people writing this poem in their own words.

Matthew Shirley (7)
Our Lady & St Werburgh's RC Primary School, Newcastle-under-Lyme

A Poem To Be Spoken Silently

It was so quiet that I heard a little boy
sip a bit of his water out of his slippery water bottle.

It was so quiet that I heard a drop of
frosty snow fall on the icy and wintry ground.

It was so quiet that I heard a breeze of
summer warm wind come through the door.

It was so quiet that I heard a young lady
put an orange hair clip in her lovely hair.

It was so quiet that I heard an old man
tie his black shoelaces.

It was so quiet that I heard a little girl
lift her yellow pencil out of her tidy pencil pot.

Megan Burke (8)
Our Lady & St Werburgh's RC Primary School, Newcastle-under-Lyme

A Poem To Be Spoken Silently

It was so quiet that I heard the soft grass sway in the cold wind.
It was so quiet that I heard warm breath coming out of my salivary mouth.
It was so quiet that I heard buzzing of electricity coming from a socket.
It was so quiet that I heard my hand raise into the invisible air.
It was so quiet that I heard the world turning this very second.
It was so quiet that I heard a splash of green paint dribble on to a sheet of paper.

Thomas Fearns (8)
Our Lady & St Werburgh's RC Primary School, Newcastle-under-Lyme

A Poem To Be Spoken Silently

It was so quiet that I heard
people fly 1,000 feet in an aeroplane
in the cold and frosty air.

It was so quiet that I heard
a hot green leaf fly
on a cold and snowy tree.

It was so quiet that I heard
a bird on a nest laying
a burning golden egg.

It was so quiet that I heard
the head gardener water
a cold and thirsty plant.

It was so quiet that I heard
James jump in the
foggy, windy sky.

It was so quiet that I heard
Marcus eat a
crunchy piece of meat.

Craig Smith (7)
Our Lady & St Werburgh's RC Primary School, Newcastle-under-Lyme

A Poem To Be Spoken Silently

It was so quiet that I heard
a big bag in the spring air.
It was so quiet that I heard
a strawberry ice cream drop in the town.
It was so quiet that I heard
a big pin drop in the snow.
It was so quiet that I heard
a goldfish talking to another fish.

Ryan O'Connor (7)
Our Lady & St Werburgh's RC Primary School, Newcastle-under-Lyme

Vampires Today

Vampires today eat veggies
Instead of sucking blood,
They like to wear yellow clothes,
And they are always being good.

Vampires tomorrow drink milkshakes,
They love to clean their teeth,
They are always picking daisies,
Their favourite food is beef.

Vampires next week
Are starting school,
They are acting like children,
They think it's cool.

Vampires next month
Are nearly out of sight,
Please don't disturb them,
Or they will give a juicy bite.

Emily Proctor (11)
St Chad's CE (VC) Primary School, Lichfield

Teletubbies Today

When you think of Teletubbies,
You think of softy things,
But actually you're wrong,
Their antennae have venomous stings.

The Teletubbies chase the rabbits
And fight each other all day,
Elbow, kick, punch each other,
And never think to play.

You would never think they'd do such things,
They really are pure bullies,
Doing ever such terrible things,
And they're really great big dummies!

Lewis Reavey (10)
St Chad's CE (VC) Primary School, Lichfield

Teachers

The teachers at my school
Are going a bit barmy,
I'm getting very worried,
'Quick, send for the army!'

They are in the staffroom,
Banging the biscuit tin,
'Quick! Get some chairs
And we can barricade them in.'

Here are the army,
Thundering in,
'They're in there,
Banging the biscuit tin.'

I sat down and said,
'Finally they've gone.'
But who's going to teach us,
Oh no! What have I done?

Beth Whitehead (10)
St Chad's CE (VC) Primary School, Lichfield

Who Am I?

Newspaper reader,
Short snoozer,
Peaceful lounger,
Football watcher,
Model fixer,
Beer drinker,
Noisy snorer,
Bike rider,
Homework helper,
Golf player,
Crazy driver,
Expert eater.

Bethany Slater (10)
St Chad's CE (VC) Primary School, Lichfield

Secrets Of The Giraffe!

Standing on its hind legs,
And playing with the kids,
As they haven't got a football
They use one of the pigs.

Diving underwater,
Going up and down,
Acting as a submarine,
Swimming all around.

As tall as a skyscraper,
As long as a house,
Eating all the vultures,
But scared of a mouse.

Those huge yellow beasts
Never have a bath,
That is why they have black spots,
Of course it's a giraffe!

Alex Jessop (11)
St Chad's CE (VC) Primary School, Lichfield

Who Am I?

Food nibbler
Floor crawler
Finger biter
Great hider
Tunnel digger
Hungry scavenger
Cupboard camper
Fruit infecter
Human hater
Fast escaper.

Steven Churchill (10)
St Chad's CE (VC) Primary School, Lichfield

Santa And How He Is Never Known

Santa Claus drives his car,
Instead of his magical sleigh.
He drops his presents at the door,
And then he drives away.

Santa messes up all the presents,
He thinks it's a real riot.
Even though he is quite thin,
He's gone on a Weight Watchers' diet.

He always wears his jet-black gloves,
And the same coloured suit.
Because he's on a diet,
He'll have to pack some fruit.

Now he's messed up all the presents
He thinks, 'I'll sort it out,'
Mrs Claus returned,
And Santa got a right shout.

Joe Dodgson (10)
St Chad's CE (VC) Primary School, Lichfield

Who Am I?

Fast runner
Carrot eater
Danger listener
Foot stamper
Hutch sleeper
Stick nibbler
Bell player
Owner lover
Face licker.

Cecilie Mortensen (9)
St Chad's CE (VC) Primary School, Lichfield

Babies Today

Just imagine if adults
Couldn't stand up or walk
Always depending on babies,
While they're teaching them how to talk.

If adults ask the babies
If they can have a pet cat,
Babies would say, 'When you're older,'
And give their head a pat.

The baby works as a solicitor,
Always going to court,
Meanwhile the adult's at pre-school,
Enjoying playtime, then being taught.

Adults get home from pre-school,
And start crying out for food,
While babies get home from a long day of work,
And stomp upstairs in a mood.

David Buckle (11)
St Chad's CE (VC) Primary School, Lichfield

Who Am I?

House cleaner,
Bath scrubber,
Brilliant cooker,
Expert shouter,
Window polisher,
Laundry washer,
Bedroom cleaner,
Coffee drinker,
Taxi driver,
Bed maker.

Jodie Whitehouse (9)
St Chad's CE (VC) Primary School, Lichfield

The Queen Today

The Queen today wears a bulldog collar,
And chews chewing gum all day long,
She goes to karate lessons twice a week,
And does breakdancing with her tongue!

Off she goes gambling at the casino,
Wearing a red leather skirt,
And holes all over her tights!
Her shoes all covered with dirt.

She makes herself lunch,
Her favourite is beans on toast,
Why don't you come round?
She's such a good host.

Rolling around the garden
With her Rollerblades on,
Exercising her favourite pet,
Oh, now where has she gone?

Rebecca Windle (11)
St Chad's CE (VC) Primary School, Lichfield

Who Am I?

Children hugger,
Food cooker,
House cleaner,
Job worker,
Tea maker,
Homework helper,
Meat cutter,
Money giver,
Good congratulator,
Sleep waker.

Ruth Morby (10)
St Chad's CE (VC) Primary School, Lichfield

Witches

Witches today are very gentle,
They never turn people to frogs,
Always wearing make-up,
Never look like some hogs.

They're always casting good spells,
People just say they're bad,
Witches bad? No, never!
But they do get a bit mad.

They cast their potions nicely,
Using flowers and maybe a butterfly,
But the parents are confused,
It makes them wonder why.

They never get into fights,
Always considerate and kind,
Always giving kids the treasures
That they find.

Sara Nock (10)
St Chad's CE (VC) Primary School, Lichfield

The Ten Sounds Of Animals

One for the growl of a large brown bear,
Two for the snuffle of a cautious hare.
Three for the scuttle of a clever spider,
Four for the roar of an angry tiger.
Five for the groan of a singing whale,
Six for the squelch of a slimy snail.
Seven for the mooing of a hungry cow,
Eight for the grunt of a peaceful sow.
Nine for the quack of a snow-white goose,
Ten for the stomp of an armoured moose.

Kimberley Monks (10)
St Chad's CE (VC) Primary School, Lichfield

Tramps Today

Tramps today wear nice clean suits,
And change them every day.
They always work hard, whatever their job,
To get a high rate of pay.

They have a huge mansion,
With a swimming pool.
They enjoy the jacuzzi,
Their life is really quite cool.

They love to go to the make-up shop,
And spend a big lump of their cheque.
They always remember to clean their teeth,
Or they will be a wreck.

Every day they have a cup of tea,
They have some toffee too.
And when they go to the toilet,
They always remember to flush the loo.

Rachel McGlade (10)
St Chad's CE (VC) Primary School, Lichfield

One For The Buzzing Of A Busy Bee

One for the buzzing of a busy bee.
Two for the itching of a naughty flea.
Three for the scuttling of a scary spider.
Four for the roaring of an angry tiger.
Five for the sleeping of a tired bear.
Six for the stamp of an angry hare.
Seven for the splash of an enormous whale.
Eight for the slither of a slimy snail.
Nine for the mooing of a milky cow.
Ten for the snoring of a sleeping sow.

Marietta Powell (9)
St Chad's CE (VC) Primary School, Lichfield

Wild Horses Today

You would think of wild horses,
Like any normal creature,
But really it's very different,
They have some quite odd features.

They stand upon hind legs,
And use artificial hands,
They bring out their guitars,
Then make up cool rock bands.

They eat their straw with forks,
And have napkins on their knee,
They wash their china dinner plates
With saltwater from the sea.

They wear clothes of all kinds,
Some even wear a hat upon their head,
In the evening they will put on pyjamas,
Then snuggle deep into bed.

Rebecca Powell (10)
St Chad's CE (VC) Primary School, Lichfield

One For The Sliding Of A Slimy Slug

One for the sliding of a slimy slug,
Two for the scuttling of a tiny bug.
Three for the buzzing of a bumblebee,
Four for the jumping of a tiny flea.
Five for the cry of a great white whale,
Six for the singing of an elegant quail.
Seven for the nibbling of a dirty rat,
Eight for the silence of a black-winged bat.
Nine for the making of a web of a spider,
Ten for the pouncing of a stripy tiger.

Jessica Green (10)
St Chad's CE (VC) Primary School, Lichfield

Wrestlers Today

Wrestlers today they never fight,
All they do is skip.
They jump up and down and leap all around,
Then they go for a kip.

They like to drink with their pinky up,
And always take small sips.
Always the fruit and never the chocolate,
And they never eat their crisps.

They always keep their teeth clean,
Never forget to brush.
Sometimes go to the toilet,
And never forget to flush!

So generally, these wrestlers
Just might . . .
Never . . .
Fight . . . !

Joseph Ali (11)
St Chad's CE (VC) Primary School, Lichfield

Wrestlers Today

Wrestlers today never, never fight,
All they do is skip and smile,
Greet each other when they meet,
And if they get scared they run a mile.

They like to eat triangle sandwiches,
And drink cups of tea,
Have a bit of sponge cake,
And cucumbers at the sea.

Their favourite pastime is knitting,
Or making daisy chains,
'The Thimbles' is their favourite programme,
They watch it while brushing their toy horse's mane.

The only shouting they ever do
Is if people can't hear their quiet voices,
'Never again,' they say will they fight,
But that's their choice.

Victoria Stanyer (10)
St Chad's CE (VC) Primary School, Lichfield

Vampires Today

Vampires today love their tea,
And love their garlic bread,
They are horrified at the thought of bats,
And are always the first out of bed.

Vampires today tuck you into bed,
Kiss you goodnight, and make you coffee,
They willingly share their sweets with you,
And are quite fond of a bit of toffee.

Vampires today go to the dentist
To have their fangs filled,
They wear the latest fashion,
And have their hair all styled.

Vampires today are committed to church,
And wear the crosses around their necks,
They like the people in the world,
And are huge fans of Becks.

Sarah Spencer (10)
St Chad's CE (VC) Primary School, Lichfield

One For The Flapping Of A Tiny Quail

One for the flapping of a tiny quail,
Two for the trail of a very slow snail.
Three for the bark of a hunting dog,
Four for the snort of a fighting hog.
Five for the buzzing of a flying bee,
Six for the tickle of a jumping flea.
Seven for the screech of a bloodthirsty bat,
Eight for the scurrying of a terrified rat.
Nine for the splashing of a hunting shark,
Ten for the squawk of a soaring lark,

Alexander Reed (9)
St Chad's CE (VC) Primary School, Lichfield

The Charge Of The Running Team

(Inspired by 'The Charge of the Light Brigade' by Alfred Lord Tennyson)

Half a mile, half a mile
Half a mile onward
Into the muddy valley
Pushed the six hundred

Charge the cross-country runners
Into the muddy valley

Forward the puddles are up ahead
'Splash through the puddles,' he said

Overtaking to the right of them
Overtaking to the left of them
Overtaking to the front of them
Pushed the six hundred
They were getting closer and closer
Across the finish line ran the six hundred.

Shaun Mann (10)
St Chad's CE (VC) Primary School, Lichfield

One For The Buzz Of An Angry Bee

One for the buzz of an angry bee,
Two for the nibble of a hungry flea,
Three for the swish of a basking shark,
Four for the tune of a singing lark,
Five for the scuttling of a crawling spider,
Six for the roaring of a pouncing tiger,
Seven for the slither of a slimy snail,
Eight for the singing of a happy whale,
Nine for the croak of a swimming frog,
Ten for the snort of a scavenging hog.

Tobias Haley (10)
St Chad's CE (VC) Primary School, Lichfield

The Charge Of The Sale Brigade

(Inspired by 'The Charge of the Light Brigade' by Alfred Lord Tennyson)

Half a checkout, half a checkout,
Half a checkout onward.
Into the Tesco valley
Barged the six hundred.
'Buy them, the Sale Brigade!
Charge for the checkouts!' he said.
Into the Tesco valley
Barged the six hundred.

Forward the Sale Brigade
Was there a bargain ignored?
Never, yet the buyers knew
There were more bargains stored.
Theirs is to bring and buy,
Theirs is not to steal or be sly.
Theirs is to *buy, buy, buy!*
Into the Tesco valley
Barged the six hundred.

Trolleys to the right of them,
Trolleys to the left of them,
Trolleys in front of them,
Rolling and crashing.
Stormed at with tomatoes and leeks,
Bargains that would last for weeks.
Into the aisles of the checkouts,
Out of the double doors,
Noble, skint six hundred.

Thomas Proctor (10)
St Chad's CE (VC) Primary School, Lichfield

Who Am I? (Kennings)

Sport watcher,
Newspaper reader,
Golf player,
Meal cooker,
Shelf constructor,
Noisy snorer,
Dog walker,
Busy worker,
Children transporter,
Short sleeper,
House tidier,
Tea drinker,
Bicycle rider,
Dish washer,
Train catcher,
Homework helper.

Louise Westoby (10)
St Chad's CE (VC) Primary School, Lichfield

Who Am I?

Meal cooker,
Sock washer,
Taxi driver,
Room cleaner,
Plate scrubber,
Vase polisher,
Loud shouter,
Toy mender,
Grass cutter,
Clothes sewer,
Present buyer,
Food shopper,
Tea drinker.

Emily Slater (9)
St Chad's CE (VC) Primary School, Lichfield

The Charge Of The Lion Brigade

(Inspired by 'The Charge of the Light Brigade' by Alfred Lord Tennyson)

Half a mile, half a mile
Half a mile onward
All in the valley of hyenas
Ran the six hundred
'Forward, the Lion Brigade!
Charge for the hyenas!' he said.
Into the valley of hyenas
Ran the six hundred.

Lions to the right of them
Lions to the left of them
Lions in front of them
Growling and snarling.
Boldly they ran and fought
In the storm of dust
Into the teeth of death
Into the mouth of Hell.

Rachel Andrews (9)
St Chad's CE (VC) Primary School, Lichfield

My Good And Bad Foods

I love lots of sprouts
With lots of salt and gravy
Yum, delicious sprouts!

I hate oranges
They have a tangy flavour
Sour oranges!

Chicken is tasty
I love it in sandwiches
Chicken is the best!

I hate onions
They make my eyes water loads
They taste like dog poo!

Sasha Bloomfield (9)
St Chad's CE (VC) Primary School, Lichfield

The Charge Of The Shopping Brigade

(Inspired by 'The Charge of the Light Brigade' by Alfred Lord Tennyson)

Half a shopping trip, half a shopping trip
Half a shopping trip onwards
Into town valley
Drove the six hundred.
Forward the Bargain Brigade.
'Charge for the clothes and shoes,' they said.
Into the valley of fashion
Ran the six hundred.

Forward the Bargain Brigade
'Keep your eyes open,' she said.
'Grab those flares,' she said.
Onward they thunder'd.

Tops to the right of them
Shoes to the left of them.
Coats in front of them
People shopping everywhere
Trying on the clothes.
Into 'New Look' shop
Ran the six hundred.

Gemma Stokes-Roberts (9)
St Chad's CE (VC) Primary School, Lichfield

One For The Squeak Of A Frightened Rat

One for the squeak of a frightened rat,
Two for the flap of a hungry bat.
Three for the screech of a soaring lark,
Four for the splash of a hunting shark.
Five for the hop of a kangaroo,
Six for the flight of a mad cuckoo.
Seven for the stamp of a flat-horned moose,
Eight for the squawk of an angry goose.
Nine for the roar of a bloodthirsty bear,
Ten for the neigh of a happy mare.

Matthew Jessop (9)
St Chad's CE (VC) Primary School, Lichfield

The Charge Of The Villa Brigade

(Inspired by 'The Charge of the Light Brigade' by Alfred Lord Tennyson)

Half a metre, half a metre
Half a metre onward
All into the valley of Villa Park
Ran the six hundred
Forward the Villa defender
'Charge for the ball,' he said
Into the valley of Villa Park
Ran the six hundred.

Forward the defender
Was there a man fouled?
'Foul! Foul!' the ref said
Someone had a broken leg
Theirs not to run and strike
Theirs but to stay on the right
Theirs not to win or lose
Into the valley of Villa Park
Ran the six hundred.

Strikers to the right of them
Defenders to the left
Goalie in front of them
Volleyed up into the goal
Villa 1-nil up
Into the hands of the
Referee, Villa scored
Six hundred.

Liam James (9)
St Chad's CE (VC) Primary School, Lichfield

Who Am I?

Golf player
Sunday lier
Fast driver
Early leaver
Fruit eater
Magazine reader
Loud shouter
Hard smacker
Dog hater
Door slammer
Huge eater
Football watcher
Loud snorer
Bad ironer
Late comer.

Laura Banks (10)
St Chad's CE (VC) Primary School, Lichfield

Seasons

Building snowmen, having fun,
Hurling snowballs, *wham!* Hit one.

Slowly moving, into spring,
Buds are growing, bluebirds sing.

Summer's coming, the weather's hot,
Run for the beach, swim a lot.

Autumn's here, falling leaves,
Trees are bare, wind deceives.

Back to winter, Christmas soon,
A brand new year, a brand new moon.

Anna Spearing-Ewyn (10)
St Filumena's Catholic Primary School, Stoke-on-Trent

Get Your Room Tidy

My mum says
'Get your room tidy.'

I'm watching TV.

My dad says
'Pull yourself together.'

I'm watching my DVD.

My mum says
'Fold your clothes up.'

I'm listening to my music.

They say
'Were you listening to us?'

I say 'No.'

Mark Holloway (11)
St Filumena's Catholic Primary School, Stoke-on-Trent

Ocean Blue Sky

Sometimes I wonder why
We have an ocean blue sky.

Sometimes I wonder why
We have to die.

Sometimes I wonder why
The birds have to fly.

Sometimes I wonder
Why, why, why, why.

Liam Cooper (10)
St Filumena's Catholic Primary School, Stoke-on-Trent

Snow

Snow is . . .
Biting at my fingers
Nipping at my toes
Maybe later I'll go sledging
Who knows?

Snow is . . .
Making me cold
And pinching my ears
My dad said he'd never like snow
Not in a million years.

Snow is . . .
Helping me and Emily
Make snowmen
Quick the boys are coming
Let's hide in the snow den.

Sally-Anne Roden (10)
St Filumena's Catholic Primary School, Stoke-on-Trent

The Eagle

See the roaming eagle flying in the air,
Soaring about without a worry or a care.
See the gliding bird,
Flying free,
A creature full of pride and dignity.
Watch now the eagle descend,
Circling down in an endless bend.
Finally, now observe it land,
With its majestic wings widely fanned.

Joshua Leech (10)
St Filumena's Catholic Primary School, Stoke-on-Trent

Peter's First Battle

At last the snow has melted,
The spell begins to break,
Peter has a job to do,
I hope he stays awake.

The wolf is out to find him, with orders from the Queen,
Let's hope the sword from Santa will help him save the day.
At the stone table, Aslan in the middle,
Tells the creatures, 'Help Peter win the fight, please move away.'

The wolf rushes to Susan,
But Peter is ready waiting.
He bravely defeats the wolf
And now the title Sir is taking.

Oliver Deakin (9)
St Filumena's Catholic Primary School, Stoke-on-Trent

My Family

Mum's in the kitchen,
Making pudding pie.
Dad's in the living room,
Watching Teletubbies.
Big boy's in his bedroom,
Trying to pass A Levels,
Nan's trying to turn the television on,
With her glasses case.
Little-un's come back from his first day at school,
With a detention.
That's my family, now tell me about yours.

Hannah McLaren (10)
St Filumena's Catholic Primary School, Stoke-on-Trent

Monday Night

On a Monday night

I don't sit down.
I don't watch telly.
I play netball.

I don't do my homework.
I don't help my mum.
I play netball.

I don't tidy my bedroom.
I don't put my clothes away.
I play netball.

I don't have my tea.
I don't help my brother.
I play netball.

Brogan Griffiths (10)
St Filumena's Catholic Primary School, Stoke-on-Trent

St Fil's

I came to St Fil's in Year 5
But my dad said it was too far to drive.

So I caught the school bus
To stop all of the fuss.

Now, I just walk to the bus stop
Which is only a short skip and a hop.

I leave the house at eight
To make sure I'm never late.

And I always get back through the door
Just five minutes to four.

I like my new school
I could almost say it's cool!

But really for me
The best thing is my rugby!

Robert Scarisbrick (10)
St Filumena's Catholic Primary School, Stoke-on-Trent

My Prayer

I go to bed every night
Put my hands together
And squeeze my eyes tight
I pray to God to bless my mum and dad
Then pray for people who are bad
And when I have finished I go to sleep
And dream of good things
In my memory to keep.
Amen.

Hannah Willis (9)
St Filumena's Catholic Primary School, Stoke-on-Trent

The Poem Of Twinkle Twinkle Little Star

(The Secret Verse)

Twinkle twinkle little star
How I wonder what you are.
With your starry glaze so bright
Will you fall out of the night,
Or will you sway until it's light?
My starry little sparkly delight.

Hazel Cross (9)
St Filumena's Catholic Primary School, Stoke-on-Trent

Snow

Snow falling from the sky,
A thick white blanket one foot high.
Children throwing snowballs,
Listen to their happy calls.
Mushy, slushy, sloppy, squelchy,
People freeze, shaking knees.

Sarah Dudley (9)
St Filumena's Catholic Primary School, Stoke-on-Trent

My Team

'Up and down, round and round
Speeds the ball on the ground.'

Where am I? Can you guess?
Watching football, I must confess.
Red and white flags wave from the crowd,
As we chant our songs out loud.
'Come on you Reds!' is what we say,
Every week on a Saturday.
I love Crewe Alex, they're the best,
We can beat all the rest.

'Up and down, round and round
Speeds the ball on the ground.'

The referee shows a red card,
A player from the other team is now barred.
Ten minutes to go, we can do it,
Steve Jones shoots, 'Oh no, he blew it!'
The score is equal, it's 2-2
And then Dean Ashton races through.
He passes, he dribbles, he takes a shot,
Yes he scored, three more points in the pot.

'Up and down, round and round
Speeds the ball on the ground.'

I'll always be an Alex fan,
For Dario Gradi is the man!

Jack Crawford (9)
St Mary's Catholic Primary School, Newcastle-under-Lyme

The Four Seasons

The world turns,
The seasons go,
The summer burns,
The winter snows.

Spring is the time when new life does start,
The grasses do sprout like velvet works of art,
The bulbs do bloom as straight as towers,
The world is awake with splendour of flowers.

Summer is the time when the sun finally shines,
When we all prepare the barbecue outside to dine,
We dream of beaches, pools and sand,
Holidays to enjoy in far, distant land.

Autumn is the time when the winds do blow,
The leaves on the trees turn golden in the sun's glow,
The animals prepare their food stores and beds,
For the long, cold days and nights ahead.

Winter is the time for the frost and snow,
The garden is asleep and nothing does grow,
The people look forward to the 25th night,
To celebrate Christ's birth, our guiding light.

The seasons have turned around,
The world has spun without a sound,
A new year is finally upon us,
And the season will turn as it always does.

Giannina Davies (9)
St Mary's Catholic Primary School, Newcastle-under-Lyme

The House Has Gone Crazy!

Mum! Mum! The cupboard's gone mad
The TV's swaying and the furniture's sad
Mum! Mum! What can we do?
We better get away before the Hoover gets you!

Mum! Mum! The iron's steaming
The bed is dancing and the rug is dreaming
Mum! Mum! What can we do?
We better get away before the Hoover gets you!

Bang! Smash! Now the light bulb's down.
Still the discs are flying and the rack's down town.
Mum! Mum! What can we do?
I am starting to go crazy and silly now too!

Mum! Mum! The desk's got your card
The carpet's driving and the box is in the yard
Mum! Mum! What can we do?
We better get away before the Hoover gets you!

Mum! Mum! The house has gone crazy
The couch is listening and the hearth is lazy.
Mum! Mum! What can we do?
Watch out! The Hoover's coming to get you.

Jessica Sellars (9)
St Mary's Catholic Primary School, Newcastle-under-Lyme

My pet

My pet doesn't have a wink
My pet's got no bark
My pet doesn't fly or sing
My pet doesn't lark
My pet is furry
It couldn't be eaten by a bat
For my pet is a purry, furry
Cutie, beauty, tiny and cuddly cat.

Katie Melling (9)
St Mary's Catholic Primary School, Newcastle-under-Lyme

Return Of The Unicorn

In the heart of the forest glade,
Where the gardener left his spade,
This silent garden which he made,
Trotting down the stone which he laid,
Rode the dainty unicorn,
The moon glowed like a pearly ring,
The stars in the sky seemed to sing,
Darkened pine trees stood bowing,
The creature's still body shining,
Raising its silver horn.

The creature gazed at the white moon,
Scents of evening seemed to loom,
The forest empty as a room,
The atmosphere enrobed in doom,
Rode the dainty unicorn,
The forest creatures still asleep,
Forest spirits come out to peep,
Looming shadows begin to creep,
The unicorn chances to leap,
Raising its silver horn.

Lydia Waszek (10)
St Mary's Catholic Primary School, Newcastle-under-Lyme

My Teacher

My teacher's really sweet,
She's always ready, she's always neat.
Wherever you see her, wherever the place,
She's always got a smily face.
She always keeps us busy in class,
Then takes us happily up to mass.
She always tries to sit us down,
Others just act like a clown.
We always try to do our best,
Normally better than the rest.

Kiera Hadgett (9)
St Mary's Catholic Primary School, Newcastle-under-Lyme

Children's Prayer

Let all the teachers in our school
Follow all the children's rules
Let them be kind and sweet
Dancing to lessons on their feet
May they not shout if we miss the bus
And if we forget our homework don't make a fuss
Forgive us if we're not on time
For after all it's not a crime

Remind our teacher if we run
We are only trying to have some fun
Let them see that we are clever
Stop them moaning about the weather
Let us sing all we like
Let us practise in Miss Moran's mic
Thank you teachers, they always try their best
Can't they tell when we need a rest?

Bethan Thomas (9)
St Mary's Catholic Primary School, Newcastle-under-Lyme

All About Me

I've got . . .
A head for nodding, shaking and thinking,
Eyes for seeing, closing and blinking.
Ears for hearing nice things and boring,
A nose for smelling, blowing and snoring.
A mouth for eating, speaking and kissing,
Teeth for chewing, but some are missing.
Arms for hugging, waving and squeezing,
Hands for helping, clapping and pleasing.
Elbows and knees are bending and stretching,
Legs are running, kicking and fetching.
And at the bottom my two little feet,
For walking and dancing and tapping a beat.

I'm pleased with my body, I wouldn't change a thing,
Except for my voice, which won't let me sing.

James McCarthy (9)
St Mary's Catholic Primary School, Newcastle-under-Lyme

The English Seasons

Spring is a time when the daffodils grow
Spring is a time when dads have to mow.
It's a time to hang out with all your friends
Everyone is so upset when spring finally ends.

Summer is fine and summer is fun
Summer is a time to sit in the sun.
You can play in the field and play in the park
And camp in the garden until it goes dark.

Autumn is a time of September weather
Autumn is a time for scarves and gloves of leather.
The leaves on the trees turn gold and red
As the squirrels make sure they are well fed.

Winter is a time of ice and snow
Winter is a time to give presents to the people we know.
Mince pies are eaten and Christmas carols sung
And in all the houses decorations are hung.

Catherine Bridgewater (10)
St Mary's Catholic Primary School, Newcastle-under-Lyme

The Wonders Of The Universe

Magical Mercury zooms through the night
Venomous Venus is misty and bright.

Earth is a place where we curl up in bed
Mars is a planet that's dusty and red.

Jupiter still has spots on its face
Saturn wears rings as it sparkles in space.

Uranus is like a gassy balloon
Neptune is as blue as a dreamy lagoon.

Pluto is tiny and turns far away
That's all the planets there's no more to say.

Jonathan Maskrey (9)
St Mary's Catholic Primary School, Newcastle-under-Lyme

What Shall I Write About?

What shall I write about?

A boat tossed on stormy seas,
Or a thunderbolt crashing through ghostly trees,
Or a ruby-red dragon with emerald eyes,
Who unfolds his ancient crackled wings
And off through the mist he flies?

What shall I write about?

Shall I write about school or friends or books,
Or silver white ghosts with petrifying looks?
Should I write about the star-studded night sky
And the planets, the moon and aliens
And a rocket that swiftly glides by?

I've got to do homework, I'm stuck, can't you see?
Tomorrow I have to give it to Miss Massey
But there is one problem there truly is,
I'm no good at poetry.

Bridget Kemball (9)
St Mary's Catholic Primary School, Newcastle-under-Lyme

A Kenning

Gentle hands
Warm smile
Tear wiper
Soft cuddles
Treat giver
Loving kisses
Story reader
Present buyer
Advice giver
Strong protector
Always there
Mum.

Erika Beeken (10)
St Mary's Catholic Primary School, Newcastle-under-Lyme

The Music Man

There was a man that played the guitar
He played it near, he played it far
In his house and in his car
Wherever he went he played the guitar.

When he got bored but not quite yet
He began to play the clarinet
He screeched so loudly he frightened his pet
I think he could find an alternative yet.

Then he saw a shiny trombone
He wanted it badly but tried not to moan
He tried it for sound that shiny trombone
But all he could do with it was groan, groan, groan.

He thought he would try his luck with the flute
It can't be difficult to blow and toot
He thought he would play it whilst wearing his suit
But even so he still got the hoot.

So back he returned to his favourite guitar
The music he played was enjoyed by afar
He became famous by playing in a bar
So these days he doesn't need to play in his car.

Joseph Jones (9)
St Mary's Catholic Primary School, Newcastle-under-Lyme

The Dragons' Doomed World

Once there was a cold and dark land,
where dragons ruled the world,
with meteors and fire balls,
from their gnashing jaws were hurled.

In that world was a *dark* wood,
where the dragons kept their evil plots,
for our world to be destroyed,
for one day they would swoop down and use their evil plans.

One day they did so,
the world was in their hands,
they set the world on fire,
to finish off their plans.

The king sent out his finest knights,
to slay the dragons' hearts,
they fought the dragons one by one,
although this is only the start.

The dragons fought back one by one,
suddenly they heard a *shout,*
their king had died a sudden death,
so they surrendered without a doubt.

Daniel Palin (9)
St Mary's Catholic Primary School, Newcastle-under-Lyme

A Knight's Tale

There was an old dragon, which lived in a cave,
Fierce and fiery he wanted a slave.
He plundered the village, and kidnapped a lass,
And took her away and tied her with grass.

There was a young knight, who lived in a castle,
Brave and bold he wants some hassle.
To fight an old dragon was his main aim,
He went out to find him some game.

The village people told him their tale,
The story slowly made him go pale.
He took a big swallow, and stood tall and strong,
If I fight this beast they'll give me a gong.

He challenged the dragon, 'Come out and fight!'
The dragon replied, 'I'm busy tonight.'
The knight burst through, into the cave.
'I'm having your head!' he began to rave.

They battled and fought with all of their might,
Blood and guts, it was a horrible sight.
The knight's strength was flagging, he started to fade,
'Please Sire for me!' shouted the maid.

He summoned his power for one final thrust,
And lunged at the dragon, his sword one last push.
Deep into its heart his sword did crunch,
'Ouch,' said the dragon, 'that's spoilt my lunch.'

'Oh thank you, Sire you are my brave night!
For thrashing the dragon in that fair fight.
Your reward shall be my hand you may wed.'
'Not likely!' he said, 'I've only one bed.'

Thomas Hamilton (9)
St Mary's Catholic Primary School, Newcastle-under-Lyme

Where Is The Sun?

'Where is the sun?' I hear you say,
Summertime left and took it away.
Looking up, the sky is grey,
A vast cold blanket shades the day.
Icy winds and battering rain,
Runs wildly down the windowpane.
Trees look bare in the frozen ground,
Where their soggy leaves are found.
Fog creeps quietly from street to street,
Padding slowly on little cat feet,
But something makes me look and stop,
A proud and delicate white snowdrop.
A thing of beauty in the wintertime,
Like a striking ray of hopeful sunshine.
A warm glow fills and makes me sing,
'Thank goodness! It will soon be spring!'

Danielle Lawton (9)
St Mary's Catholic Primary School, Newcastle-under-Lyme

Have you Ever Seen . . . ?

Have you ever seen a fish in an army tank?
Have you ever seen a bank filled with money?
Have you ever seen a night riding on a horse?
Have you ever seen a bed in a sea?
Have you ever seen a sea looking around?
Have you ever seen a pear wearing shoes?
Have you ever seen a sail on a boat?
Have you ever seen someone putting a deer on a letter?
Have you ever seen a rock recording a record?
Have you ever seen a tree bark coming out of a dog?
Have you ever seen some hair hopping around?

Siân Smith (10)
St Mary's Catholic Primary School, Newcastle-under-Lyme

The Age Of The Dinosaur

Tyrannosaurus, the meat-eating dinosaur
Powerful body, legs, sharp teeth and more.

Ankylosaurus, his club on his tail,
His shell is deadly and strong, sharp as a nail.

Allosaurus, a meat-eating horror beast.
He'll tear you apart and make your his feast.

Diplodocus, the longest dinosaur ever known.
A plant-eating herbivore, a forest was its home.

Carboniferous period is where it began.
300 million years ago amphibians ran.

Triassic period the first dinosaurs appeared.
The reptiles had been around 100 million years reared.

Jurassic was when lush vegetation grew.
The dinosaurs were plentiful and some even flew.

Cretaceous was the heyday of the dinosaur.
Hundreds of different kinds lived more and more.

Caenozoic era was after the death of them all.
Mammals took over 65 million years ago or more.

Today one mammal dominates the Earth, man our friend.
A scary beast, the brain, the wit, the cause of war and the end.

Adam Sutton (9)
St Mary's Catholic Primary School, Newcastle-under-Lyme

Raven Poem

Ravens, ravens, cool
Little play things
They have enormous wings
They don't like it when they sting.

The raven's claw,
It just makes violence and gore,
It's so sharp it's nearly against the law.

The raven's wing,
It hits you with a sting.
The sound it makes is 'cling',
Yes that's the raven's wing.

The raven's head,
At night sleeps in a garden shed,
With its body attached to it,
It is left to go in the garden shed.

The raven's body,
It's very mouldy,
It's proud and strong,
Good enough to win,
The best raven's body
In the shell.

The raven's foot,
When moving makes the sounds of clut
It's good for ticking and also picking.

Lewis Emanuel (10)
St Mary's Catholic Primary School, Newcastle-under-Lyme

Ghosts

They rush past you like a gust of air,
You never know where they might lair,
If you see them they will give you a scare,
If I were you I would *beware!*
The ghosts, the ghosts of the haunted castle.

They play their ghostly tricks on you,
The only way to escape is if you know what to do,
Their plans are evil and if it's played on you you'll cry 'Boo hoo!'
If I were you I would face it's true,
The ghosts, the ghosts of the haunted castle.

Run, run before you die,
Otherwise your body will just lie,
Your soul will fly up to the sky
And you'll become a *ghost* that's why!
Run, run from the ghosts of the haunted castle.
Ooohh!

Niamh Flynn (10)
St Mary's Catholic Primary School, Newcastle-under-Lyme

Snowy Weather

The snow is cold and soggy
The snow is like some paper
The snow is turned to snowmen
The snow is turned to snowballs

The snow is a fun thing
The snow is turned to icicles
The snow has covered everything
And put black ice on the road

The snow is frosty and bitter
The snow makes people sneeze
The snow is fun weather.

Liam Tomlinson (11)
St Paul's CE Primary School, Stafford

Rainbow

The clouds were milky and dreamy
The sky was like a balloon
Full of imagination
There is nothing you can do!

The raindrops were like see-through crystals
The sun was luminous and bright
Full of consideration
There is nothing you can do!

This object is really beautiful
This object is really bright
Full of imagination
There is nothing you can do!

Its shining colours are blinding
It's really quite immense
Full of consideration
There is nothing you can do!

The rainbow hits the sky so hard
The rain falls out of the sky
The rainbow sets people's hearts on fire
Then the rainbow suddenly dies!

Gemma Campbell (11)
St Paul's CE Primary School, Stafford

The Twister

He twists around without a sound.
He manufactures hatred through the land.
He never can be outmanned.
He never can contain his rage
When he is released from his cage.
He stores his anger up
And then leaps up.
He opens his fiery eyes
And starts to rise.

Aiden Hickman (10)
St Paul's CE Primary School, Stafford

The Rain

The rain goes pitter-patter as the storm brews up
You can hear cars going through the puddles
And making a big splash!

Dog shaking their warm fluffy coat
The black clouds gathering together
As if they are cold and there comes a downpour of rain.

Raindrops in the sky stop and start to drizzle
And then a cloudburst of rain and everybody is inside again.

Garden pots breaking and people looking out of the window
In astonishment as their garden is in such a disgrace.

Everybody locks their front door as they go out
And just hope it doesn't rain, cars won't start,
Window wipers on and off they go.

All the shops are shut and nobody is about,
The street lights have turned off and nobody is around.

The storm stops and the lights are off in every street
Then there goes somebody's bin, the storm is black.

Grace Stokoe (10)
St Paul's CE Primary School, Stafford

Storm

Watch out a storm is coming
Hide in your houses
Hide anywhere
Storms are scary striking everywhere
The storm is almost here
Run as far as you can
And watch the lightning light up the sky.

Jack Harding (10)
St Paul's CE Primary School, Stafford

The Sun

She is golden,
Glistening in the sky,
Standing proudly very high.

Her bronze rays
Touch the ground,
As she gracefully twirls round and round.

She brings smiles to faces,
Laughter to streets,
As she magnificently shines.

She is very old,
But never loses her beauty,
Her glisten or her shimmer.

The day goes by,
The sky turns darker,
She'll come back tomorrow,
But for now it's goodbye.

Lauren Carroll (10)
St Paul's CE Primary School, Stafford

The Terrible Tornado

He roared into the valley at the speed of a jet
He can appear out of thin air just to cause chaos.
He comes and goes as he pleases.
He can come and go in the blink of an eye.
He is as great as a tank but as light as a feather.
He is more powerful than the wind and the rain.
he is the most terrifying thing.
He is a tornado, a very deadly thing
And if you are to see him
Be sure to shout
Help!

Robert Ross (10)
St Paul's CE Primary School, Stafford

Bing Bang The Snow Is Falling

Bing bang the snow is falling
There's a white sheet on the ground
Bing bang the snow is falling
There's snowballs flying around
Bing bang the snow is falling
There are snowmen being built
Bing bang the snow is falling
Everyone's got no guilt
Bing bang the snow is falling
The windows are all frozen over
Bing bang the snow is falling
Nobody is sober
Bing bang the snow is falling
The air is really chilly
Bing bang the snow is falling
All the children are really silly
Bing bang the snow is falling
There is peace within the home
Bing bang the snow is falling
No one can hear a single moan
Bing bang the snow is melting
It is nearly all gone
Bing bang the snow is melting
'Bedtime now,' says Mum
Night night.

Alexandra Foden (11)
St Paul's CE Primary School, Stafford

Thunderstorm

As it starts to rain some people think it will be nice,
but they could soon change their mind,
the rain starts to get heavy, soon you get a thunderstorm,
the rain pours down and waters plants,
the lightning strikes trees and buildings,
the thunder crackles and booms and bangs,
people and animals are frightened to be
caught in this monsoon weather and heavy showers,
as the storm continues to shower everything
the lightning starts to get dangerous
it starts to hit people!
The trees are getting blown about
by the powerful wind and struck by lightning
watch out of their windows at the pouring rain,
the cracking thunder, the flashing lightning
and the blowing wind.
As the rain gets heavier, the farmer's crops get ripe,
but the storm has caused a lot of damage
to the environment and the people are not happy
then the rain stops,
the wind stops
everything stops,
the clouds clear
and the sun comes out,
the storm has ended.

Jamie Andrews (9)
St Paul's CE Primary School, Stafford

The Sun

As the day starts the sun will rise
Over the towering mountains
Gleaming proudly
With its sparkling colour
Like a flaming fire
But beware, because when the clouds come out
They will block out the sun
And the skies grow grey
The sun then battles its way
Through the sky to come out again.

With its burning rays it makes
The best of brilliant days
That's why the sky is always blue on sunny days
At the end of the day
The sun will go down
Making the sky go a wonderful tropical colour
Then at the end of an exhausting day
The sun will go down
And that means that the day has finished.

Joycelyn Smith (10)
St Paul's CE Primary School, Stafford

The Sun Is Making Me Burn

The sun is making me burn,
It is making me burn till I crisp,
I'm having frosty cold drinks
And shivery chocolate ice cream.
I sat in the shade
A bit cooler than out.
I fell asleep
And made my mum shout.

Nicole Seaman (10)
St Paul's CE Primary School, Stafford

The Snow

Freezing snow
soft
slippery snow
creeps
from winter to winter
as white as a swan
as wet as water
fun to play in
freezing snow.

James Stanley (10)
St Paul's CE Primary School, Stafford

The Wind

Last night I heard the wind creeping in and out.
Blowing against all the windows smothering all the candles out.
Short-circuiting all the wires.
Rolling car tyres.
Loudly whistling through the night.
Giving up a massive fight.
But now it is morning it has gone.

Joseph Owen (10)
St Paul's CE Primary School, Stafford

Friday 13th February I Was So Quiet . . .

It was so quiet that I heard a centipede wriggle across the dirty floor.
It was so quiet that I heard the sunlight sparkle on the snowy grass.
It was so quiet that I heard frying pans sizzle as I fried a fishy egg.
It was so quiet that I heard the wall screech as I hammered in
a pointy nail.
It was so quiet that I heard the hair come through another millimetre
on the baby's shiny head.

Heather Wakefield (8)
St Thomas' CE (A) Primary School, Stoke-on-Trent

The Seaside

The seaside is sparkling turquoise
and shiny gold.
It tastes like minty ice cream
and an orange ice lolly.
It sounds like the waves
crashing into the rocks.
It looks like light blue and orange
floating in the fresh air.
It smells like sizzling hot dogs
and juicy chips.
It makes me feel free!

Emily Whittaker (8)
St Thomas' CE (A) Primary School, Stoke-on-Trent

The Seaside

The seaside is bright yellow with golden sand.
It tastes like the salty sea and strawberry ice cream!
It sounds like the ice cream van coming
And the splashing waves.
It looks like the lovely light blue waves
Splashing everywhere and the children having lots of fun.
It smells like the lovely vanilla ice cream and the sea.
It makes me feel great inside.

Charlotte Bowcock (8)
St Thomas' CE (A) Primary School, Stoke-on-Trent

The Seaside

The seaside is grey and brown.
It tastes like strawberries.
It sounds like seagulls.
It smells like bananas and grapefruit.
It smells like berries.

Julie Anne Jones (7)
St Thomas' CE (A) Primary School, Stoke-on-Trent

It Was So Silent . . .

It was so silent I could hear
A cuddly cloud shiver in the sky.
It was so silent I could hear
An ant crawling in the sand.
It was so silent I could hear
A bird flying in the sky.
It was so silent I could hear
A snail sliding across the grass.
It was so silent I could hear
A spider spin a web.

Eloise Litherland (8)
St Thomas' CE (A) Primary School, Stoke-on-Trent

The Seaside

The seaside is a nice and relaxing place.
It tastes like sand and salmon.
It sounds like seagulls shouting and the wind blowing.
It looks like a big glass of water and strips of string inside.
It smells like fresh air and salty water.
It makes me feel like jumping in and splashing.

Hollie Bolton (7)
St Thomas' CE (A) Primary School, Stoke-on-Trent

The Seaside

The seaside is colourful and light blue.
It tastes like gold and rock.
It sounds like seagulls.
It looks like porridge in a bowl.
It smells like a river and some honey.
It makes me feel perfect and happy.

Victoria Robinson (8)
St Thomas' CE (A) Primary School, Stoke-on-Trent

Snow White's Pocket

A purple bow.
A small Barbie doll.
A ring as big as her finger.
A letter from her father.
A photograph of her mother.
Some bright nail polish.
A wooden pyramid toy.
A pink headband.
A rosy, big, red apple.
A big orange comb.

Paige Buckley (7)
St Thomas' CE (A) Primary School, Stoke-on-Trent

The Seaside

The seaside has sandy yellow and lots of sparkly blue.
It tastes like ice cream and lollies.
It sounds like waves crashing together.
It looks like paradise.
It smells like fresh fish from the freezer.
It makes me feel special.

Jack Williams (8)
St Thomas' CE (A) Primary School, Stoke-on-Trent

It Was So Silent . . .

It was so silent I could hear shooting stars in space.
It was so silent I could hear televisions on in the houses.
It was so silent I could hear the sea swishing from far away.
It was so silent I could hear the air blowing.
It was so silent I could hear bacteria chipping.

Hannah Wootton (8)
St Thomas' CE (A) Primary School, Stoke-on-Trent

Ten Things Found In A Queen's Pocket

A golden shiny crown.
Some jewels as nice as the sky.
A bowl of custard creams.
A spoon with the initials on it EQ.
A silver feather with a golden pen underneath.
Some golden cloth to cover up her shiny head.
Some shiny silver glass on the windows.
A cushion to go on the golden throne.
A shiny golden watch.
A shiny plate with a golden roast dinner.

Emma Bowers (8)
St Thomas' CE (A) Primary School, Stoke-on-Trent

The Seaside

The sea is blue and yellow and peach.
It tastes like lollies and ice cream.
It sounds like the waves are going to crash.
It looks like sand and water.
It smells like water and the waves splashing on the rocks.
It makes me feel free.

Jonathan Keeling (8)
St Thomas' CE (A) Primary School, Stoke-on-Trent

The Seaside

The seaside is light blue and yellow.
It tastes like fish flowing in the air.
It sounds like waves washing you away.
It looks like a beautiful place to be.
It smells like salmon fish.
It makes me feel happy and fit.

Emily Jane Lowndes (7)
St Thomas' CE (A) Primary School, Stoke-on-Trent

My Home

Home is yellow.
It tastes like eggs.
It sounds like cats miaowing.
It looks like peace and joy.
It smells like cats.
It makes me feel happy.

Bethany Hope Yates (7)
St Thomas' CE (A) Primary School, Stoke-on-Trent

School

School is multicoloured.
It tastes like sprouts and pickled onions.
It sounds like a drum kit.
It looks like a bomb site.
It smells like teachers' smelly shoes.
It makes me feel happy.

Daniel Jenner (8)
St Thomas' CE (A) Primary School, Stoke-on-Trent

The Seaside

The seaside is yellow and light blue.
It tastes like rock.
It sounds like the waves.
It looks like mud.
It smells like flowers.
It makes me feel joyful and wonderful.

William Haynes (8)
St Thomas' CE (A) Primary School, Stoke-on-Trent

The Seaside

The seaside is light blue and shiny yellow.
It tastes of salty air and greasy chips.
It sounds like a bride.
It looks a tip.
It smells like hot dogs.
It makes me feel happy.

Demi McKinney (7)
St Thomas' CE (A) Primary School, Stoke-on-Trent

The Seaside

The seaside is blue and yellow.
It tastes like ice cream and hot dogs.
It sounds like blue waves.
It looks like swimming.
It smells like fish.
It makes me feel happy.

Rachel Mullock (7)
St Thomas' CE (A) Primary School, Stoke-on-Trent

The Seaside

The seaside is yellow and light blue.
It tastes like cool water and ice cream.
It sounds like birds singing and waves moving.
It looks like the ocean singing and birds making noise.
It smells like the breeze moving.
It makes me feel free.

Jordan Jones (8)
St Thomas' CE (A) Primary School, Stoke-on-Trent

The Seaside

The seaside is yellow and light blue.
It tastes like ice cream and milkshake.
It sounds like birds flying past.
It looks like paradise.
It smells like salt.
It makes me feel happy.

Jordan Hackney (8)
St Thomas' CE (A) Primary School, Stoke-on-Trent

Home

Home is bright blue and yellow.
It tastes like a Galaxy bar.
It sounds like the birds singing.
It looks like a comfy bed.
It smells like a chocolate bar.
It makes me feel happy!

Matthew Hayes (7)
St Thomas' CE (A) Primary School, Stoke-on-Trent

The Seaside

The seaside is yellow and light blue.
It tastes like jelly and ice cream.
It sounds like seagulls.
It looks like it's summer.
It smells like a sip of hot cocoa in the morning.
It makes me feel happy and good!

Courtney Baskeyfield (8)
St Thomas' CE (A) Primary School, Stoke-on-Trent

Slide Or Glide?

Mice squeak
Lions leap
Parrots squeal
Snakes peel
Horses jump
Elephants clump
Kangaroos jump
Camels slump
Jellyfish wobble
Dogs gobble
Eagles glide
Frogs slide
Birds tweet
But
I sleep!

Melissa Grocott (8)
Silverdale Primary School

Jump Or Slump?

Frogs leap
Beetles creep
Camels slump
Rabbits jump
Lions roar
Larks soar
Squirrels climb
Slugs slime
Koalas climb at a different time
But
I drink lime!

Leona Nicklin (8)
Silverdale Primary School

Cheat Or Beat?

Cheetahs cheat
Lions beat

Elephants charge
Bulls barge

Lark soars
Bee wars

Monkey swings
Racoons cling

Snakes camp
But
I stamp!

Bethan Plant (8)
Silverdale Primary School

Wiggle Or Jiggle?

Worms wiggle
Bugs jiggle
Birds fly
Frogs die
Mice creep
Deer leap
Cats are small
But
I am tall!

Rhian Goodridge (9)
Silverdale Primary School

Jump Or Jiggle?

Lions roar
Magpies caw
Elephants large
Mice charge
Pigs crawl
Wolves call
Chicks thump
Camels slump
Hedgehogs whirl
Worms curl
Horses run
But
I won!

Dean Culverwell (8)
Silverdale Primary School

Dash Or Smash?

Leopards dash
Turtles smash
Cows stare
Mammals glare
Crabs snap
Starfish slap
Cheetahs sleep
Deer leap
Frogs jump
But I hum!

Zachary Husnu (8)
Silverdale Primary School

Strike Or Bite?

Snakes strike
Crocodiles bite
Scorpions sting
Birds wing
Jackals creep
Kangaroos leap
Bees sting
But
I sing!

Joshua Bailey (8)
Silverdale Primary School

Bark Or Lark?

Cats purr
Birds chirp

Dogs bark
Lions lark

Butterflies fly
But
I lie.

Chelsie Pritchard (9)
Silverdale Primary School

Chase Or Race?

Cheetahs chase
Lions race
Elephants eat
Leopards leap
Birds fly
But
I cry.

Sam Birchall (8)
Silverdale Primary School

The Magic Fish

I caught a fish in the sea,
It was a multicoloured fish,
It was the right size for my dish,
I grabbed it by the tail,
But then I saw a whale.

The next day
I saw that fish,
I caught it and it said,
'I'll grant you a wish,
If you let me go'
So I let him go but,
I got no wish.

I caught him again,
He said the same,
But I took him back to my house,
He went in the pan,
On to the plate
And he tasted delicious.

Benjamin Oliver Poole (9)
Silverdale Primary School

Hop Or Stop?

Guinea pigs squeal
Monkeys peel

Dogs smoke
Cats joke

Ants small
Zebras tall

Elephants stop
But
I hop!

Alexandra Bester (8)
Silverdale Primary School

Jump Or Slump?

Frogs leap
Beetles creep
Camels slump
Rabbits jump
Lions roar
Larks soar
Squirrels climb
Slugs slime
Koalas climb at a different time
But
I drink lime!

Chloe Mountford (8)
Silverdale Primary School

Dash Or Smash?

Leopards dash
Turtles smash
Cows stare
Mammals glare
Crabs snap
Starfish slap
Cheetahs sleep
Deer leap
Starfish float
But
I don't.

Joshua Walker (9)
Silverdale Primary School

Valentine

It's soon Valentine's Day
You just go your way
Because I said:

'Be mine my love
Because Valentine will soon
Wed me and you
For you are my love and these flowers for you.'

As the rhyme goes:
'Roses are red,
Violets are blue,
Sugar is sweet and so are you.'

That is us on Valentine's Day,
So go your way.

Rebekah Lewis (10)
Silverdale Primary School

Wiggle Or Jiggle?

Dogs bark
Seagulls go, 'Ark, ark!'
Elephants walk
Parrots talk
Zebras bang
Horses clang
Frogs jump
But
I clump!

Jade Robinson (9)
Silverdale Primary School

Bite Or Fight?

Snakes bite
Lions fight

Owls howl
Wolves prowl

Elephants bang
Bats fang

Spiders spin
But
I win!

Jack Hulme (8)
Silverdale Primary School

Weathers

This is the weather the dogs like
And so do I,
Where the hikers hike,
And birds fly,
And the little robin has a rest,
And the children get undressed,
And the children do their best,
And take a test,
And so do I.

Jonathan Hughes (9)
Silverdale Primary School

Jake Said

Jake said,
'Sometimes teachers try to teach you.
But people never listen to you.'
Then the teacher asks you,
'Do you know what you are doing?'
And you say,
'I do not know.'
'Well you'd better listen more.'
In the end she shouts, 'Get to Mr Beech.'

Jake said, 'Teachers really do teach you a lesson.'

Jake Smith (10)
Silverdale Primary School

The Fellowship

Strider king of Gondor
And heir to Isengard

Other people call him Aragorn
Son of Arathorn

Legolas prince of Mirkwood
To surrender to Orcs he never would

Legolas and his Mirkwood bow
Always loves a shining rainbow

Gimli son of Gloin
Cousin of Baliin

Gimli swings his axe
Gives Orcs great big smacks.

James Ackerley (10)
Silverdale Primary School

Poppy Day

P eace has come at last
O ur fight is over
P oppies appear after the war
P eople heartbroken
Y ears of bangs

D ays go by
A ll love you
Y ou and me are safe now.

Hannah Martin (10)
Silverdale Primary School

Animal Poem

'Woof' went the pig
'Baa' went the hen
'Hee-haw' went the cat
Who went slipping on a mat.

'Hobble, gobble' went the sow
'Cheep, cheep; went the cock
'Tu-whit tu-whoo' went the foal
Running in the pen.

'Cock-a-doodle-doo' went the lion
'Quack, quack' went the turkey
'Cluck' went the tiger
Playing like mad.

Thomas Grand (10)
The Richard Heathcote Primary School

What Is Yellow?

Yellow is a sunrise
Blazing and bright
Yellow is a lovely rose
Is that right?
Yellow is a banana
It smells lovely and ripe.
Yellow is lemonade
It's sharp and sour.
Yellow is the hot sand
Burning my feet.
Yellow is a show off
No doubt about it,
But can you imagine
Living without it?

Annie-Mae Smith (7)
The Richard Heathcote Primary School

Alien Spacecraft

Frightened maybe?
Slightly amazed
Brightly shining
A spaceship!
A spaceship!

Lightly hovering
Around and around
A friendly alien shouts,
'Come out and play.'
What do I say?
'OK!'

Joshua Eardley (7)
The Richard Heathcote Primary School

Mum Rapper

(Based on 'Gran Can You Rap?' byJack Ouseby)

Mum was in her garage she was fixing her lamp,
When I tapped on the door to see if she could rap.
'Mum can you rap? Can you rap? Can you Mum?
And she dropped down her tools and said to me,
'Son, I'm the best rapping mum this world's ever seen,
I'm a slit slat, slop slap, rap rap queen.'

And she jumped from the bench and from the room
And she started to rap with a bing bang boom
And she rolled up her sleeves and rolled round her head
And as she rolled by this is what she said,
'I'm the best rapping mum this world's ever seen,
I'm a drop drop, trip trap, rap rap queen.'

She rapped past my cat and rapped past my father,
Before she saw me she saw my little brother.
Her rapping was great but I don't care,
She's the best rapping mum this world's ever seen
She's a slit slat, slop slap, trip trap, drip drop, rap rap queen.

Adam Bloor (10)
The Richard Heathcote Primary School

The Aliens That Came To Earth

One dark night
I got up for a drink
I heard a strange noise
Coming from the garden
I saw lights!
I saw . . .
A UFO flying low
An alien was shouting at me
'Will you come out and play?' it said
What could I say
But OK!

Aaron Holt (8)
The Richard Heathcote Primary School

Nonsense Poem

There is a moon that is shaped like a spoon,
The woman is weird but she has a big beard,
The chimp speaks to you,
'Baa,' said the kangaroo,
The dog goes, 'Quack,' with the shirt on his back,
'Woof, woof,' goes the duck,
As we ate our dinner we were told to brush our teeth,
As we did maths we wrote a story,
Mr Pen told us to pack up
So we put him in a wardrobe and locked the door,
As we went outside to play we read a book,
As we did gymnastics we all sat down and talked,
As we did art we experimented with gas,
As we did ICT we went to play.

Jack Harvey (10)
The Richard Heathcote Primary School

Crazy Class

Children telling teachers what to do.
As we did games we got out our books and pencils.
As we ate dinner we were told to brush our teeth.
As we did maths we wrote a story.
Mr Pen told us to pack away
So we put him in a wardrobe and locked the door.
As we played outside we began to read.
As we did gymnastics we all sat down and talked.
As we did art we did experiments with gas.
As we did ICT we all went out and played.
As we got to school we went back home again.

Kyle Kennedy (11)
The Richard Heathcote Primary School

At Night When It Is Dark

At night when it is dark
and I am in bed
and I can't get to sleep
I hear noises.

I hear click, click, click
I know what it is
it's the boiler
but I pretend it's the monster's jaws clicking
as he comes to eat me
and I hide under the covers.

At night when it is dark
and I am in bed
and I can't get to sleep
I hear noises.

I hear shoo - shoo - shoo
I know what it is
it's the wind
but I pretend it's a ghost coming to my room
and I run into my mum's bedroom before it gets me.
At night when it is dark
and I am in bed
and I can't get to sleep
I hear noises.

At night when it is dark
and I am in bed
and I can't get to sleep
I hear noises.

I hear creak, creak, creak
I know what it is
it's the stairs
but I like to pretend it's a robber
coming to steal my teddy bear
so I hide it under my bed.

Then I begin to yawn - ahh, ahh
I'm so tired
I fall asleep
and dream! Zzzz.

Lucy Amphlett (8)
The Richard Heathcote Primary School

Mr Copnall

Mr Copnall is a cool blue
He is a warm spring afternoon
He is a busy football pitch
He is a big ball of sun
And a football strip
A bouncy chair
He is A Question Of Sport
And a bowl of ice cream.

Harriet Maddock (10)
The Richard Heathcote Primary School

My Mum

She is a bright yellow
On a warm spring day.
She is a wide open field.
She is a sunny sunbeam.
She is a pair of shoes.
She is a tall lamp.
She is a DIY programme.
She is a healthy salad.
She is my mum.

Laura Peers (11)
The Richard Heathcote Primary School

Animal Poem

'Miaow' went the dog
'Woof' went the cat
'Oink' went the horse
Sleeping on the mat.

'Hobble-gobble' went the owl
'Moo' went the duck
'Cheep, cheep' went the foal
Running in the meadow.

'Quack, quack' the turkey cried
'Cock-a-doodle-doo' went the lion
'Hee-haw' went the chickens
Playing really mad.

Nicola Phillips (10)
The Richard Heathcote Primary School

In Dream Country

In dream country,
Nothing's quite the same.
Everybody and everything are so tame.
Animals would talk to you,
But would be in pairs of two.
Pretty flowers would grow
And there'd be a land called Pho.

Megan Tyler (7)
The Richard Heathcote Primary School

Beauty -Tanka

Beauty was my bird
She always hated Bertie,
She was quite noisy,
Dad buried her in a bin,
She is always in my heart.

Leighan Anckaert (9)
The Richard Heathcote Primary School

'Woof' Went The Sheep

'Woof,' went the sheep
'Oink,' said the cow
'Moo,' said the cat
Running through its dog flap
'Hobble, gobble,' said the dog
'Pop' went the cat's ear
'Roar,' went the donkey
'Baa,' said the horse
'Cluck,' said the sow
'Bow-wow,' went the fly
Flapping its wings
'Miaow' went the lion
'Cock-a-doodle-doo,' went the tiger
'Roar,' went the ladybird
'Cheep, cheep,' went the turkey
'Wolf, wolf' went the pig flapping its wings.

Elliott Amphlett (9)
The Richard Heathcote Primary School

'Woof' Said The Donkey

'Woof,' said the donkey
'Moo,' said the hen
'Quack,' said the little dog
Running in the den.

'Hee-haw,' said the pig
'Croak,' said the goose
'Cheep, cheep,' said the horse
Eating a moose.

'Cock-a-doodle-doo,' said the cat
'Roar,' said the moose
'Baa,' said the ant
Looking at the goose.

Zachary Stanier (10)
The Richard Heathcote Primary School

The Silly School

As we went to play football
We put rounder bats out.
As we went swimming
We put our ballet suits on.
We went on the Internet
And wrote up our maths.
We went to do PE but
We did our RE instead.
As Miss went to play her piano
She went on her electric guitar.
As I peeled my banana
I ate an orange.
When we were going home
We went back to school.
As we did woodwork
We made a metal chair.

Gavin Smith (10)
The Richard Heathcote Primary School

Nicola

Nicola is brown
She is a cold winter morning
In a freezing playground
She is an ice cube on a wall
She is a school uniform
And a tidy desk
She is Countdown
And a bowl of bangers and mash.

Sophie Lambeth (11)
The Richard Heathcote Primary School

The Wobbit Wout

You may have never heard of the Wobbit Wout,
It has four legs and a long blunt snout.
Tiny ears and a multicoloured body,
It never gets dirty or ever muddy.
Small pink tongue and leathery skin,
Never ever finds food in a bin.
It eats little insects, maybe ants,
No clothes for ants in their pants.
It lives in a cave with pointed rocks,
It even has a door with many locks.
You may have never heard of the Wobbit Wout,
But just look out for the long blunt snout.

Hebe Louise Gill (9)
The Richard Heathcote Primary School

Haiku - Susie Pet

She sharpens her nails
She sleeps on my mum's warm bed
She wins all her fights.

Cory Burgess (9)
The Richard Heathcote Primary School

Sam - Haiku

I loved her so much,
She still remains in my heart
Died in the year '03.

Charlotte Holt (9)
The Richard Heathcote Primary School

Dragon Heart

I stared up coldly
What did I see?
I saw a fierce dragon
Flapping at me.
But fear not, for he was kind
But all the bad things
Dwelled in my mind.

I dreamt of claws, razor-sharp
Creeping around in the dark.
The skin I felt was as cold as night
But as worse as any, his fierce bite!

He flapped up dust
With his giant wings.
The fire he breathed
Melted things.

He gave me the ride of my life
And at the end offered me a tooth-like knife.

I went home that night
And went to bed
Looked out of the window and said,
'Little dragon, little dragon,
What do you plea?
Would you like to be best friends with me
And look above the clouds so bright
In the cold and frosty night?'

The next day my eyes lit
What a dream
Or was it?

Daisy Turnbull (11)
Thomas Barnes Primary School

The PlayStation Night

My PlayStation is a luxury
It brings out the best of me!
Up and down my spaceship goes
Shooting down my alien foes.
Bing, bing, bong, bong
Complete a game, I'm in song!
Switch the game, racing now!
Race over fields, seeing cows!
I lose a game against my dad
Now I'm feeling really sad.
Not to worry, I'll thrash him next turn
Then I'll make him learn!

Up the stairs, into bed
And put the pillow on my head.

Jake Turnbull (11)
Thomas Barnes Primary School

Why

Why do people shout?
Why do people hit?
Why do people spend, spend, spend?
Why do people shop?
Why do people do nothing?
Why do people act innocent?
Why do people lie?
Why do people nag?
Why do people blame?
Why do people cheat?
Why do people hate?
Because that's what people do, including you.

Jade Hastings (10)
Thomas Barnes Primary School

Disappointment

They promised me some snow,
One day off school I wanted
But did I get that? No.

Disappointment filled my heart,
As I looked out the window,
They promised me, *promised!*
Tears ran down my cheeks, but still no snow came.

Then as I was going to school,
A little spark of hope was given
As the snow came slowly down.
But did not last for long as it
Melted on the ground.
Then later the snow came down,
And heavy it was this time,
And stayed on the ground,
So out we went to play.

Anna Keight (10)
Thomas Barnes Primary School

My Cat

My cat is gentle and bright,
She likes to come in and sleeps through the night.
The only time she's a silly cat
Is when she comes in and attacks the mat.
She miaows and wails an awful lot,
She really has lost the plot.
The nicest thing of all
Is when she's curled up in a ball.
And there she stays all snuggled and warm
Until she gets a meal call.

Jade Spencer (10)
Thomas Barnes Primary School

Along The Canal

A canal boat goes along
Smoke rising out of the pipe,
Swaying in the water
All quiet during night.

On the footpath the leaves are crunchy
All different colours they are,
There's gold and brown, yellow and red
Well that's what the teacher said.

In the distance you can hear
The army guns going off,
When you get closer they get louder
And then you can see the red flag going up.

In the way horse poos lie
All smelly and sloppy,
People step into them
And get their shoes all messy.

Catherine Beniston (10)
Thomas Barnes Primary School

Who Needs Parents?

Who needs parents?
All they do is nag
Do this, do that . . .
God my life's a drag.
Always moaning,
They haven't got a clue,
I think I'm getting too old to listen to you!
When I'm alone I spend hours on the phone
Yacking to my friends, before the 'oldies' come home
But when they see the bill
Guess who they're gonna kill?

Jemma Holland Knight (11)
Thomas Barnes Primary School

What Am I?

Here it comes
The big gust
Blows at my hair
The wind, of course.

Here it comes
The big chill
Freezes my nose
The snow, of course.

Here it comes
The big heatwave
Roasts my body
The sun, of course.

Jaye Coulson (10)
Thomas Barnes Primary School

I love Saturday

Why do I love Saturday?
It's my dancing day!
Every week is something new,
So much fun - just great to do!

I love my leotard,
And shiny tap shoes.
I just love dancing
To the music
Rock and roll, classical
Or rhythm and blues.

Zoe Kirk (8)
Thomas Barnes Primary School

Henry, My Dog

Henry is cute,
But when he's in the way we call him a galloot.
When a train comes rumbling past,
He runs away very fast.

When Henry drinks his water,
He spills at least a quarter.
You know when Henry wants to eat,
Because he hangs around your feet.

When Henry runs and plays,
He acts like he can do it for days.
When Henry sees a wet log,
He makes sure it doesn't smell like another dog.

Jacob Kirk (10)
Thomas Barnes Primary School

In The Woods

Squirrels rushing from
Tree to tree collecting acorns,
The sneaky squirrels trying
To hide themselves for hibernating.

Tree tops swaying
Side to side,
The tree trunk standing
Strong and proud.

Sweet, small songbirds
Flying high over the trees.

Samuel Lloyd (9)
Thomas Barnes Primary School

Boat Trip

We're on a boat trip
Round the world
Sailing on the sea
In our boat playing games
We're going out for tea.

We're on a boat trip
Round the world
Sailing on the sea
Playing in the open air
Oh no, I've been stung by a bee.

We're on a boat trip
Round the world
Sailing on the sea
Lots of dolphins
Swimming around me.

We're on a boat trip
Round the world
Sailing on the sea
Lots of seals around
And no, I'm in the sea.

Robert Gilbert (10)
Thomas Barnes Primary School

My Day At School

I start a new day at school.
On the playground I talk and play.
Me and my friends are being cool.
'Into school!' the whistle blows to say.
My lessons are good but hard.
Maths is my favourite of them all.
In art we make a Christmas card.
I look out the window to see snow fall.

Steven Taft (9)
Thomas Barnes Primary School

My Mum!

My mum has got black hair,
Always has, always will,
She only plays recorder,
And her nickname's Diamond Lil.

She usually wears joggers,
She likes to feel at ease,
Although she is quite bossy,
She is easily pleased.

Great as great can be is she,
The greatest ever found,
She does sing quite a lot though,
It is quite a lovely sound.

She is the greatest in the world,
Her brown eyes show spirit true,
My mum is the best I say,
I love her, yes I do.

Sophie Thomas (10)
Thomas Barnes Primary School

Autumn

I love to conquer
All my friends
I fight and fight
Until it ends.

Red, brown and golden leaves
Lots of colours,
For me and you.

I climb my nan's tree
Hoping there's a conker for me.

Jonathan Mandefield-Green (11)
Thomas Barnes Primary School

Footy Crazy

Jessica is my name
Football is my game
I gave up all my dancing
And my mom thinks I am insane

I play in the rain
I play in the sun
I play in the mud
Which is lots of fun

I play at home
I play away
I just can't
Wait for Saturday.

Jessica Arrowsmith (9)
Thomas Barnes Primary School

My Rabbit

I have a rabbit,
His name is Dill,
He loves to eat grass,
Cos it gives him a thrill.

He loves the garden,
He loves to hop,
He has his own lead,
So I take him round the block.

He likes his food,
His treats too,
He'll come inside,
And gnaw on your shoe!

Philippa Allan (11)
Thomas Barnes Primary School

My Pets

I have got two dogs
Called Sam and Bert
Sam is pretty bright
But Bert is a bit of a twerp.

Sam fetches sticks
And likes to go out,
Bert lies around
And likes to do *nowt*.

Sam loves to swim
And have lots of fun,
Bert loves to eat
And lie in the sun.

Now Sam is old
And has had to slow down,
But Bert is just the same
Still a bit of a clown.

Mia Fisher (8)
Thomas Barnes Primary School

Shreader

I had a dog called Shreader
He died, he died,
Mom said he was asleep
She lied, she lied,
And now that my dog is dead
I am very, very upset
But now I'll get a new pet
I wish that my cat had died instead.

Jonathan Phillips (10)
Thomas Barnes Primary School

Attack Of The Pirates!

A group of pirates sail the ocean looking for treasure
They pillage all the villages on the ocean shore
They are vicious thieves who sail in a great flagship.

Their captain is a foul man who does nothing but count his gold
He has expensive clothes which he has bought with his riches.

They attack with cannons and swords to get to the much wanted treasure
Only a handful of people survive their ambush.

I survived the attack of the pirates will you?

Stephen Manton (10)
Thomas Barnes Primary School

What I Like

Joe is my name
My brain is insane
I love sweets
Especially treats

I love PlayStation games
Especially planes
I never hate
Especially my mates.

Joe Jackson (9)
Thomas Barnes Primary School

There Was A Young Dog Called Floss

There was a young dog called Floss
Who always thought she was the boss
She went for a walk
And started to talk
Now she really is the boss.

Sophie Blincoe-Allsop (10)
Thomas Barnes Primary School

Nan!

I'm football crazy
I'm chocolate mad
I go to my nan's
And she's always
Glad!

She brings me chocolate
She brings me sweets
She brings me candy
Which is always
A treat!

Nan reads my book
She's a wonderful cook
My nan is great
She's my best mate!

Ross Bennett (9)
Thomas Barnes Primary School

My Pet Gus

My pet Gus has a Mohican on his back
He is big and fat and eats grass
He is black and white and brown
Has big claws

My pet Gus goes to play in the run
He is quite slow at walking
He is a good pet
He has got small ears

My pet Gus likes running but he can't
He likes dandelions
He tries to get out
He likes to have fun.

Danny Henry (8)
Thomas Barnes Primary School

My Pet Stan

My pet Stan is very naughty
He climbs trees
And he guards the food
He hisses at other cats
And he's very fat

He hasn't got a tail
And he jumps off the fridge
He jumps out of the window

He's a mad cat!

Thomas Ellis (9)
Thomas Barnes Primary School

My Magic Box

(Based on 'Magic Box' by Kit Wright)

I will treasure in my box . . .
A red ruby and a diamond from a magical fairy queen,
The glow from an angel's halo,
A scale from a magical mermaid's tail.

I will treasure in my box . . .
The magical spell from a witch's wand,
A dolphin jumping with its team in the glittering sunset,
A feather from Pegasus' golden wings.

My box is decorated in different glittery magic
From a witch's wand,
With the sunset surrounding it
With the glow of the moon and stars at night,
And the brightness of the coloured rainbow.

I will fly in my box,
Around the world,
Around the glow of the golden beach.
I will fly around space,
I will keep on flying until my wings wear out.

Alice Williams (11)
Walhouse CE Junior School

My Magic Box

(Based on 'Magic Box' by Kit Wright)

I will conceal in my box . . .
The white gleaming hair off a first-born horse's tail,
The gem off God's own ring from His left forefinger,
And the bark of the second female dog running in the sky.

I will conceal in my box . . .
The drop of blood shed by Christ when He was crucified,
A newly-born kitten's twinkle from its eye,
And a Greek god's headpiece worn on his death day.

My box is designed from a killer whale's shimmer,
Pearls from the bottom of the Antarctic Ocean,
And the tiny glittering pendant of 50 alien species.

I shall hide in my box . . .
A dolphin in the crashing waves of the Pacific,
And be found by beautiful talking animals.

Paige How (11)
Walhouse CE Junior School

My Magic Box

(Based on 'Magic Box' by Kit Wright)

I will capture in my box . . .
a golden sun that only people loyal to God can see,
a kingdom from Heaven with no pain or death,
a newborn baby with its weak cries.

I will capture in my box . . .
the sweet drink that makes humans immortal,
the rich scent of a poppy alone in a field,
and the bright colours of a phoenix rising from the ash.

My box will be constructed of the shining scales of a colourful fish,
the handle will be made of emeralds glimmering in the summer sun,
the hinges will be made with platinum and a diamond to secure it.

In my box I shall glide like a bird over the lands
and keep precious stones from thieves and criminals.

Bryony Gooderidge (10)
Walhouse CE Junior School

My Magic Box

(Based on 'Magic Box' by Kit Wright)

I will store in my box . . .
A crystal lake that shines like coloured glass in a window,
The soft humming of a bee hovering on a breath of wind,
And the bright twinkle of a star on a dark black night.

I will treasure in my box . . .
The face of a lady weeping by a stream,
And a young bear cub sleeping by its mother,
And the lush green colours on tropical rainforest trees.

My box is created from pixie dust, snow and volcanic lava,
With enchantments and secrets in every corner,
And the hinges are spiderwebs joined by a soft thread.

I shall rule in my box,
Be queen and explore the lands,
Then sleep in my seaweed bed,
Under the moon in the grassy forest.

Grace Hollins (10)
Walhouse CE Junior School

My Magic Box

(Based on 'Magic Box' by Kit Wright)

I will place in my box . . .
The first snowflake to fall in winter
The last leaf to fall in autumn,
And the unexpected eruption of a dormant volcano.

I will place in my box . . .
The first shine of the Northern Lights
The last roar from a dying dinosaur
And the final gasp of the last man on a dying earth.

My box is made from gleaming sapphires and glistening rubies.

I will travel in my box to lost lands and ancient cities.

David Jackson (10)
Walhouse CE Junior School

The Magic Box

(Based on 'Magic Box' by Kit Wright)

I will treasure in my box . . .
A golden sunset over the desert going down over the sand,
A beautiful tear of a dying animal shimmering in the sun,
Cheers from a party on Christmas Day.

I will treasure in my box . . .
The lightning bolts from a thunderous storm,
The noise of raindrops falling on a roof,
And the cry of a newborn baby.

My box will be fashioned from hot lava
And the finest silk ever, diamonds and gold,
And the colours of a rainbow.

I shall skate in my box down Mount Everest,
And I shall ride through the Atlantic Ocean
On a dolphin's back then rest ashore in the sun.

Joshua Wilson (11)
Walhouse CE Junior School

My Magic Box

(Based on 'Magic Box' by Kit Wright)

I will lock away in my box . . .
A shiny star from the moonlit sky,
The first tear from a newborn baby's eye,
And the last bark before an old dog dies.

I will lock away in my box . . .
The crystal splash from a dolphin,
The highest note of an opera singer,
And the snowdrop from Mount Everest.

My box is fashioned by feathers of a golden eagle's wing,
Red rubies from my grandmother's necklace,
And a pearl from the clearest sea.

I shall swim in my box on the back of a killer whale
Over the Pacific Ocean.

Bryony Wort (11)
Walhouse CE Junior School

The Magic Box

(Based on 'Magic Box' by Kit Wright)

I will capture in my box . . .
The blast from a wizard's ivory wand,
Old Trafford on a hectic match day,
And the shot from a deserted blaster.

I will capture in my box . . .
The crash of a streak of lightning,
A paperboy in a UFO,
And an alien on a bike!

My box is created from silver, diamond and snow,
With sparks on the lid and flames in the corners,
And the hinges are the teeth of dragons.

I shall run through my box on the 50m running track,
Then fly through the sand of the long jump pit,
And get a new world record!

Nick Baker (10)
Walhouse CE Junior School

My Magic Box

(Based on 'Magic Box' by Kit Wright)

I will treasure in my box . . .
A blond blade of David Beckham's hair,
And numbers from the lovely world of math,
Also a feather from a golden eagle.

I will treasure in my box . . .
The first snowball of winter going down your back,
The pull of your brake when riding your bike down the street,
Getting pulled into your Harry Potter books because you're engrossed.

My box is designed by wood shaved bark off a tree,
With the leather off a football casing,
And each corner will have the names of my true best friends.

I will swerve my football in the top corner in my box
And I will jump the sea's waves on a jet ski in Barmouth.

Jack Mancicius (11)
Walhouse CE Junior School

My Magic Box

(Based on 'Magic Box' by Kit Wright)

I will treasure in my box . . .
a horn from a newborn unicorn,
a glow from an angel's halo,
and a scale from a mermaid's tail.

I will treasure in my box . . .
a dolphin jumping and dining in the sunset,
a grey thoroughbred galloping around his field,
and a feather from the wing of Pegasus.

My box is decorated in shining stars,
and is sprinkled in a princess' fairy dust.
It is plastered in gold and silver,
and it is wearing magic jewels.

I will journey in my box,
through the sky and the sea,
and I will land gracefully,
on a golden beach.

Scarlett Ward (11)
Walhouse CE Junior School

Pollution Haikus

People drop litter
It destroys animals' homes
What a disaster.

We pollute the air
Smoke coming out our chimneys
Making the air smell.

What about the seas?
The oil spillage kills creatures
Stop the pollution.

Melissa Martin (10)
Walhouse CE Junior School

My Magic Box

(Based on 'Magic Box' by Kit Wright)

I will conceal in my box . . .
An ivory tusk from a golden elephant,
The volcanic Io from Planet Jupiter,
And a diamond swan from Baramere.

I will conceal in my box . . .
A crystal star from a bleak winter's night,
The whicker of a stallion
Leading his herd to a cool, clear stream,
And the mythical horse, Pegasus,
From the land of ice and snow.

My box is created from ice, glass and snow,
With hinges of silver and steel,
With pixie dust on the lid
And fairies in the corners.

I will gallop on my horse in my box
Into a forest deep, lush and green,
And come out on a mountain top,
With dew drops glistening all around.

Alicia Skelton (10)
Walhouse CE Junior School

The Magic Box

(Based on 'Magic Box' by Kit Wright)

I will capture in my box . . .
A glimmer of the golden sun,
The laugh of a newborn baby,
And the last goodbye from the one you treasure.

I will capture in my box . . .
The lightning bolts from the thunderous storm,
A snowy Christmas and a New Year's Day,
And all the magic from the heavens above.

My box is created from silver and gold locks
To keep my treasures safe,
Blue steel with violet hinges,
And all the love for my family.

I shall travel in my box to the land
Of Narnia to meet Aslan,
And dance with joy when I get there.
Then I will end up at home
With the sun coming through the window
Like nothing happened.

Michelle Keeley (10)
Walhouse CE Junior School

My Magic Box

(Based on 'Magic Box' by Kit Wright)

I will treasure in my box . . .
A diamond from a brand new glittering necklace,
A glow from a golden eagle,
And a shiny star from a beautiful sky.

I will treasure in my box . . .
A feather from a bird flying by,
A laugh from a newborn baby boy,
And lava from my lava lamp.

My box is fashioned
With stickers of dolphins and killer whales,
Gold and silver diamonds,
And colourful long rainbows.

I shall swim in my box,
I shall sing full of grace in my box,
And will play my games all day!

Jessica Jones (10)
Walhouse CE Junior School

My Magic Box

(Based on 'Magic Box' by Kit Wright)

I will capture in my box . . .
The red moon on a sunset evening
A golden spark from a sparkling sun
And the first man to touch beautiful dark blue water.

I will capture in my box . . .
The last word of a dying uncle
A fiery flame from an exploding volcano
And a touch of a first kitten's whisker.

My box will be made from . . .
Golden icicles from faraway lands
With glittering moonlight pictures
And its joints will be made from silver slate.

I will journey in my box to faraway lands
I will journey in my box to Atlantis
Then wash away in the deep blue sea
And finally end up on a lovely golden beach.

Jordan Lockett (10)
Walhouse CE Junior School

My Magic Box

(Based on 'Magic Box' by Kit Wright)

I will capture in my box . . .
The silver moon that shines light at night,
The first glimmer of the sun in summer,
A bird building its nest from danger.

I will capture in my box . . .
The howling of a werewolf,
Signalling to others that danger is about,
A brave knight in silver shining armour,
The most terrifying rumour ever to be told and spread.

My box is fashioned with . . .
Gold gleaming stars,
A piece of the shining sun,
And the colours of a colourful rainbow.

I shall travel far, far away,
To the lands of the unknown,
Unknown to mankind.

Reece Beeston (11)
Walhouse CE Junior School

My Magical Box

(Based on 'Magic Box' by Kit Wright)

In my magical box I will treasure . . .
A shimmer of a newborn baby's tear
The glow of a flickering fire
The glittering of the star as it wanders longingly
Around the Milky Way

In my magical box I will treasure . . .
The laughter of children on the first winter morning
The soft velvet touch of a fluffy white cloud
The opening of new poppy petal
Awakening from its deep sleep.

My magical box is like the pirate's treasure
My magical box is the colours of the rainbow
The sound of the longing moan of a whale.

I will hide in my box in the depths of the shadows
I will mix in my box the wildest of dreams
In my box I will soar to the ends of the world.

Natasha McCulloch (11)
Walhouse CE Junior School

My Magic Box

(Based on 'Magic Box' by Kit Wright)

I will treasure in my box . . .
The rough skin of an enchanted rhino
the dance of a forgotten tune long ago
a leap of an emerald frog shining in the sunshine . . .

I will capture in my box . . .
The gentle breeze of a summer day
a smooth dolphin swishing beneath the waves
and a fairy queen dancing around leaves

My box is fashioned from . . .
A charmed butterfly's wings
and the angel's magic dust
a witch's cackle
and a song from a luscious evergreen wood!

I shall shine in my box with the fireflies of the night
and swing around the tall trees like a monkey
then I shall close my box and seal it
with a pink starlit ribbon
my magic box.

Amelia Tizley (11)
Walhouse CE Junior School

My Magic Box

(Based on 'Magic Box' by Kit Wright)

I will treasure in my box . . .
The ocean's shimmer, captured in a sapphire,
A dolphin's crystal splashes, as it jumps.
The wind's whisper, rustling through the trees.

I will treasure in my box . . .
The yelps of joy from a newborn puppy,
The first bell to ring in a new school term.
The frost's bite of the winter breeze

My box is cut from long black silk
Like a black Labrador's coat,
As black as the night and dark as coal.
A padlock so no one will peep in and see
My heartfelt desire,
And the hinges of a knight's almighty armour.

In my box I will run around as free as a bird,
I will swim away like a killer whale.
Then, I'll just sleep.
Arrgh! Peace!

Charlotte Begg (10)
Walhouse CE Junior School

My Magic Box

(Based on 'Magic Box' by Kit Wright)

I will treasure in my box . . .
An extract from an everlasting story
A crystal from a glittering glacier
And a tail feather from a phoenix.

I will capture in my box . . .
The rubbery smile of a sleek dolphin
A last electricity spark from a worn TV
And the first step of a learning child.

My box is created from the tin from an old tin soldier,
And conkers from an old twisted tree,
Finished with five rings made for the elves of Rivendell.

I shall ride the land in my box on a white pearly unicorn
And see ships setting off to an unknown land
Under the light of a purple moon.

Verity Tizley (11)
Walhouse CE Junior School

My Magic Box

(Based on 'Magic Box' by Kit Wright)

I will keep in my box . . .
The first flight of a baby bird
The last conker from a dying tree
The sounds and sights of the world.

I will keep in my box . . .
A soldier on the back of a white swan
And a fairy on top of a green tank
The slap of the sea on a seaside sunset.

I will create my box from . . .
Pearls and dreams with jewels put in
With carvings on the lid and gold round the edges
And hinges made from a million clams.

I shall sail the seven seas in my box
I shall wander the world and beyond in my box
I shall see all that is to be seen in my box.

Nathan Read (11)
Walhouse CE Junior School

My Magic Box

(Based on 'Magic Box' by Kit Wright)

I will capture in my box . . .
A dream from a lonely child,
A swimming pool from the hottest country,
And a flower from a beautiful garden.

I will capture in my box . . .
A rainbow from a magical world,
A polar bear from Norway's coldest desert,
And a tropical fish from the Pacific Ocean.

My box is decorated in . . .
Pictures of dolphins and starfish
Diamonds as shiny as silver panels
And a wooden frame from a bathroom mirror.

In my box I will . . .
Swim in my water park
Ski in my snowdrome
And I will live freely until the lid closes.

Alicia Pearce (10)
Walhouse CE Junior School

My Magic Box

(Based on 'Magic Box' by Kit Wright)

I will treasure in my box . . .
The first firework of a Chinese new year,
The exploding fire of an erupting volcano,
And a shiver on a cold winter's night.

I will capture in my box . . .
The first goal of football history,
The first word of the English language,
And the first cry of a newborn baby.

My box is designed with the smoothest
Silk from India,
The fancy symbols of China
And the finest gold from a dark gold mine.

I will surf in my box . . .
The great huge waves of the Atlantic Ocean,
I will ride the first dinosaur that ever existed,
And I will slide down Mount Everest
On a shiny sledge.

Thomas Newman (10)
Walhouse CE Junior School

My Magic Box

(Based on 'Magic Box' by Kit Wright)

I will treasure in my box . . .
A grain of sand from the bottom of the ocean
A leaf from a tree in the garden of Eden,
And a frosted ring of the moon.

I will treasure in my box . . .
The eye of a screaming storm
The first leaf to fall in autumn
And the moonlit rings of the planet Saturn.

My box is carved from oak and is decorated with pearls,
Its corners are plated with gold
And hinges are shimmering ivory.

In my box I will . . .
Travel around the world
And collect even more things.

Thomas Evans (11)
Walhouse CE Junior School

My Magic Box

(Based on 'Magic Box' by Kit Wright)

I will treasure in my box . . .
A diamond worth a million pounds,
The golden glow from a sunlit beach.
The tooth of a Sabre-toothed tiger.

I will store in my box . . .
The soul of a dragon
A feather of a phoenix
The snowy peak of a mountain.

My box is created from bronze, oak and gold,
It is decorated with the finest silver and pictures
Of moonlit nights, dragons and fish with multicoloured scales.

Its hinges are made of jade and ruby,
I will journey to countries, worlds and planets,
Adventure to never-found islands and countries - in my box.

Christian Pepper (10)
Walhouse CE Junior School

January Snow

Snowflakes are white, softly falling to the ground,
Hedges are hairy, they stand weakly
Bricks are brickly, they broke deeply,
Woolly sheep stand lonely,
Playground covered white, smoothly across,
Squirrels run and hide up trees,
Birds all fly home.

Abigail Anslow (10)
Woodseaves CE Primary School

Garden Shadow

When we moved to Woodseaves End,
Every afternoon at five,
An unearthly wind would come
The dead would come alive.

Then would come a shadow,
Past the twisted tree,
Past the garden meadow,
Then she would walk straight past me.

She picked our garden flowers
From our garden lawn,
Then she would carry them
In her basket which was torn.

Amie Moore (10)
Woodseaves CE Primary School

Winter Snow

W inter's here, so is the snow
I ndoors the women moan, 'It's too cold.'
N ext door there's a snowball fight.
T hen comes the cursed sun,
E verything's melted,
'R ight, who broke my window?'

'S am did it!'
'N o, I didn't!'
'O h for heaven sake let's get outta here!'
'W ait until I get my hands on you kids!'

Timothy Buckless (10)
Woodseaves CE Primary School

The Haunted Mansion

Never go in the haunted mansion
'Cause you won't come out again!
Don't try to escape, it is just in vain
Don't listen to what it says
It just tells lies!
Try not to look at its dark eyes,
Or at its cloak -
Is it a woman or a bloke?
'Cause it has its silly little ways
It has wrinkles so it must be old
No, well it might!
Oh this house is so cold -
Does it like children?
No, it puts them in jars and glues on the lids.
How long has it been here?
Who knows?
I'll tell you something, I bet it wouldn't mind a cold beer.

Chloe Josephine Hampton (9)
Woodseaves CE Primary School